Computer Fundamentals

Windows Edition

Kevin Wilson

www.elluminetpress.com

Computer Fundamentals: Windows Ed

Images used with permission. Wackerhausen, RainerKnäpper, KDS4444, monsitj, HLundgaard @ iStock. Mnyjhee @ Dreamstime. Luminescent Media / CC-BY-SA-3.0

Publisher: Elluminet Press
Director: Kevin Wilson
Lead Editor: Steven Ashmore
Technical Reviewer: Mike Taylor, Robert Ashcroft
Copy Editors: Joanne Taylor, James Marsh
Proof Reader: Robert Ashcroft
Indexer: James Marsh
Cover Designer: Kevin Wilson

eBook versions and licenses are also available for most titles. Any supplementary material referenced by the author in this text is available to readers at

www.elluminetpress.com/resources

Table of Contents

About the Author 9

Acknowledgements 11

The Computer 12

Types of Computer 13
    Desktop *13*
    Desktop: All-in-one *14*
    Laptop *15*
    Netbook *16*
    Chromebook *17*
    Tablet Computers *18*
    Hybrids *19*
Computer Components 20
    CPU *20*
    Memory (RAM) *21*
    Hard Disk *22*
    Motherboard *23*
    Expansion Slots *24*
    Sound Card *25*
    Video Card *26*
    Screens *27*
    Resolution *28*
Decoding the Jargon 29
    Computer Specs *29*

Peripherals 32

Printers Types 33
    Inkjet Printer *33*
    Laser Printer *34*
Installing Printers 36
    HP Printers *36*
    Epson Printers *38*
    Canon Printers *39*
    Brother Printers *39*
    Add Printer to Windows 10 .... *40*
    If you're Struggling to Connect your Printer *41*
        WPS *41*
        Enter WiFi Network on LCD Panel *42*
        Older Printers *42*

Connect using USB 45
Connect Using Ethernet 45
Download the Printer Drivers 46
Managing Printers 48
Print Problems 49
Mouse 50
Adjustments 51
Using the Mouse 51
Left Click 52
Double Click 52
Right Click 52
Scroll Wheel 53
Touch Pad 53
Left Click on Something 54
Right Click on Something 54
Scroll 55
Keyboards 55
Function Keys 56
Modifier Keys 56
Flash Drives & External Drives 57
External DVD Drive 59
NAS Drives 61
Other Peripherals 62
Data Ports 63
USB 63
USB-C 64
Ethernet 65
FireWire 65
ThunderBolt 66
eSATA 66
Video Ports 67
DVI 67
HDMI 68
VGA 68
Component Video 69
Composite Video 69
Audio Ports 70
1/8" (3.5mm) Phono Jack 70
1/4" (6.35mm) Phono Jack 70
RCA Audio 71

Computer Software **72**

The Operating System..73
Running Windows the First Time 74
   Regional Settings 74
   Terms Of Use 75
   Connect to your WiFi 75
   Enter WiFi Password 76
   Sign in for the First Time 76
   Set a PIN Code 77
   Link your Phone...77
   Set up OneDrive...78
   Meet Cortana 78
   Do More with your Voice...79
   Location 79
   Find my Device...79
   Send Diagnostic Data 79
   Improve Inking & Typing 80
   Get Tailored Experiences with Diagnostic Data 80
   Let Apps use Advertising ID 80
The Windows Desktop 82
   Desktop Anatomy 82
   Start Menu...82
   Task Bar...84
      Anatomy..84
      System Icons 85
   Action Centre 85
   Timeline Activity History...87
   Windows Search..88
      Searching for Files 89
      Searching for Apps...90
      Searching for Windows Settings 91
      Narrowing Down the Search 91
   File Explorer...92
      Home Ribbon...93
      Share Ribbon...93
      View Ribbon...93
      Organising your Files..94
      Creating Folders..95
   Moving Files...96
   Copying Files...97
Apps & Applications 98

Installing Apps..*99*
Installing Software *100*
Some Useful Software *101*
   Google Docs...*101*
   Google Sheets..*101*
   Google Slides...*102*
   Libre Office..*102*
   GIMP..*102*
   Audacity..*102*
   Zoom..*102*
Software Compatibility *103*
Un-installing Software..*105*
Resetting Apps..*108*
Start-Up Programs *109*
Arranging Windows on Desktop 110
   Moving a Window *110*
   Resizing a Window *111*
   Minimise, Maximise & Close a Window....................*112*
   Window Snap Feature..*112*

Internet Security **114**

Malware...115
   Virus *115*
   Worm *115*
   Trojan *115*
   Rootkit *115*
   Ransomware *116*
   Spyware *116*
Social Engineering...117
   Phishing..*117*
   Pharming *118*
   Pretexting...*118*
   Shouldering *119*
   Tech Support Scams *119*
   Fake Popup Messages...*119*
Threat Prevention 120
   Biometric Measures *120*
   Strong Passwords...*120*
   2-Factor Authentication *120*
   Public Key Cryptography.......................................*121*
   Firewalls..*122*
   Routers *122*

Anti-Virus Software 123
    Windows Security 123
    Avast 124
    AVG 124
    Dealing with Infections.................................... 125

Using the Internet **126**

Getting Online 127
    DSL 127
    Fibre Optic 128
    Cable 130
    Satellite... 131
    3G/4G/5G.. 131
Browsing the Web 132
    Google Search.. 134
    Web Addresses.. 134
    Bookmarks Bar.. 136
    Add Website to Bookmarks Bar 136
    Organising the Bookmarks Bar 137
    Browsing History... 139
    Finding Files you've Downloaded 140
    Printing Pages... 141
    Extending Chrome 142
Using Email.. 143
    Web Based Mail... 143
    Windows Mail App... 143
        Adding your Email Accounts 144
    Reading Mail.. 147
    Mozilla Thunderbird 148
Cloud Computing 150
    The Cloud 150
    OneDrive.. 152
    Google Drive.. 153

Backing Up **156**

Creating a Local Backup.. 157
    Setup 157
    Scheduling Backups 161
    Restoring Files 162
Google Drive 163
NAS Drives 167

Common Problems..**168**

   Computer Won't Turn On 169

   Keyboard or Mouse not Working 170

   Computer Freezes...171

   Windows Wont Start 171

   PC Boots Slowly..172

   Slow PC 172

   No WiFi 175

   Recovery Mode..179

      Entering the Recovery Environment *179*

      Safe Mode...*181*

      Startup Repair *183*

      Restore Point..*184*

      Re-install Windows..*185*

   System File Check 187

   Startup Programs 188

   Drive Optimisation...189

   Disk Cleanup..190

Further Reading **192**

Index...**194**

About the Author

With over 20 years' experience in the computer industry, Kevin Wilson has made a career out of technology and showing others how to use it. After earning a master's degree in computer science, software engineering, and multimedia systems, Kevin has held various positions in the IT industry including graphic & web design, programming, building & managing corporate networks, and IT support.

He serves as senior writer and director at Elluminet Press Ltd, he periodically teaches computer science at college, and works as an IT trainer in England while researching for his PhD. His books have become a valuable resource among the students in England, South Africa, Canada, and in the United States.

Kevin's motto is clear: "If you can't explain something simply, then you haven't understood it well enough." To that end, he has created the Exploring Tech Computing series, in which he breaks down complex technological subjects into smaller, easy-to-follow steps that students and ordinary computer users can put into practice.

Acknowledgements

Thanks to all the staff at Luminescent Media & Elluminet Press for their passion, dedication and hard work in the preparation and production of this book.

To all my friends and family for their continued support and encouragement in all my writing projects.

To all my colleagues, students and testers who took the time to test procedures and offer feedback on the book

Finally thanks to you the reader for choosing this book. I hope it helps you gain a better understanding of computers.

The Computer

These days, computers come in various shapes and sizes. You can get desktop PCs, laptops and tablet computers.

In this section, we'll take a look at the different types of computers that are available, as well as the components that make up a computer.

We'll try to decode some of the common jargon you might hear when using a computer.

Types of Computer

You can get desktop PCs, laptops and tablet computers, as well as netbooks, chromebooks, and hybrid computers that are a cross between a tablet and a laptop.

Desktop

The traditional desktop computer with a monitor, computer case, keyboard and mouse. Can either be a Mac or a PC.

These machines are usually quite big and have the most computing power. They are aimed at gamers, graphic designers, video editors, office users and professional users. They are ideal with large screens, plenty of computing power and storage space.

Desktop computer sales for home users have been steadily declining in favour of laptops and tablet computers.

Desktop computers still seem to have a place in an office environment, however this seems to be slowly changing toward a cloud based environment where data is stored on the cloud and accessed using laptops or tablets.

Desktop: All-in-one

This type of desktop is virtually identical to the traditional desktop we talked about above, except the computer case has been done away with.

Instead, all the internal hardware (processor, RAM, hard disc and video card) from the computer case, is integrated into the back of the screen itself.

This makes the whole system easier to set up, as all you need to do is plug in your keyboard and mouse, hook it up to the power and you're ready to go.

Some of these systems have touch screens built in, allowing you to tap icons on the screen instead of using a mouse.

Apple's iMac was the first to use this format, but many other manufacturers have copied this design.

Laptop

A typical laptop computer, also sometimes called a notebook. This one is a laptop running Windows 10.

Laptops usually have a similar spec to their desktop counterparts, however there are some compromises due to space. They tend to have less RAM and run slightly slower than desktops. The screens are usually between 12" and 17".

They can run all the software and apps that are available on a desktop and come with Windows 10 or Mac OS.

The major advantage of a laptop, it its portability. The fact that you can use it in any room, sit on the sofa and surf the web, talk to your friends. Or do some college work in a coffee shop or library.

With laptops, you can plug in various peripherals such as a mouse as well as an external screen or projector. This makes them ideal for those who do public speaking, teaching/lecturing, and presentation.

Some laptops nowadays even include touch screens where you can navigate around the screen by tapping icons and menus rather than using a mouse or trackpad.

Netbook

Netbooks are small cut down versions of laptops. They have less RAM, HDD space and are designed to be small, lightweight and inexpensive which makes them great for carrying around.

The screens are usually about 10". Notice the size compared to the ball point pen in the photograph.

Netbooks can run Windows 10, some form of Linux or even Chrome OS.

These are great for working on the go or travelling around. They can run traditional software such as Microsoft Office and work well when browsing the web, social media or keeping in touch via email.

These have limited power, so anything more processor intensive such as Creative Suite or some types of games will struggle to run on these machines.

These machines also have limited storage space, so if you have a lot of music, documents, videos, or photographs, you'll quite quickly run out of space.

Most of these machines can be used with some kind of cloud storage such as OneDrive or GoogleDrive.

Chromebook

A ChromeBook is a laptop or tablet that runs an operating system called Chrome OS and uses Google's Chrome Web Browser to run web apps. Chromebooks don't run Windows.

At its core, Chome OS is a linux based operating system and will run on hardware with either intel/amd x86/64 or ARM processors.

ChromeBooks are designed to be used online, meaning you must be connected to the internet all the time whether you are at home, the office, in school, college, the library, or generally out and about. Without an internet connection, your ChromeBook can still function but will be limited at best.

Traditional software such as Microsoft Office, Adobe Creative Suite and many types of games do not run on these machines. However, Google have developed their own alternatives. Instead of Microsoft Office, you'd use Google Docs.

You can also download countless apps from the Google Play Store for all your other software needs from social media and communication, to getting your work done.

Tablet Computers

Tend to be a cut down compact version designed with touch screens. This one is running Windows 10 in desktop mode.

Examples of these come in the form of iPad, Microsoft Connect Tablets, Surface Tablets, Samsung Galaxy Tab, Amazon Fire and many more.

These are ideal for travelling and carrying about as they are light weight and can be stored in your bag easily.

They have countless apps available from the app store that you can download directly onto your tablet. These range from games to cut down versions of Microsoft Office and basic graphics packages. They are also good for browsing the web, social media, making video calls and keeping in touch using email.

Some tablets can even run traditional software, if they are running Windows 10.

Hybrids

Hybrids are a cross between laptop computers and tablets. An example of a hybrid is Microsoft's surface tablet.

These can function as a laptop and have detachable keyboards. Once you detach the keyboard you can use the device in tablet mode, attach the keyboard and you can use it as a laptop.

These devices aren't usually as powerful as traditional laptops and are usually smaller and light weight.

They also have countless apps available from the app store that you can download directly onto your hybrid. These range from games to cut down versions of Microsoft Office and basic graphics packages. They are also good for browsing the web, social media, making video calls and keeping in touch using email.

Some hybrids can even run traditional software, if they run Windows 10.

Computer Components

A computer is made up of various components that work together to make the up the machine.

CPU

Also known as the processor, the CPU is the component that responds to all the commands you give the computer. The job of the CPU, is to execute a sequence of stored instructions called a program. The program could be an app, a web browser, or a software application such as Microsoft word.

There are two main CPU manufacturers: Intel and AMD. There are various different CPUs, each running at different speeds and manufactured for different computers such as laptops, desktops, or tablets. Each manufacturer has their own specs, names and series for their CPUs. This is where things get a bit confusing. There are a lot of different processors out there with different numbers and series. However it all boils down to a few numbers to take note of. I've highlighted these in bold. Lets take a look at some common ones.

Intel Pentium / Celeron. These chips are common in cheap laptops, and offer the slowest performance, but can handle tasks such as web browsing, email and document editing. You'd be better off spending a bit extra and going with a Core i3 or i5.

Intel Core i3. Performance is about entry level for basic computer usage such as web browsing, email, social media, word processing, music and looking at a few photos.

AMD A, FX or E Series. Found on low-cost laptops, AMD's processors provide decent performance for the money that's good enough for web browsing, internet, email, streaming films or tv, photos and music, as well as word processing etc.

For example:

> AMD **A6**-9220 APU 2.5GHz
> AMD Quad-Core Processor **FX**-9830P

Intel Core i5. If you're looking for a mainstream laptop with the best combination of price and performance, get one with an Intel Core i5 CPU. Always make sure the model number ends with a 'U', HK, or 'HQ' - these offer better performance. For example:

> Intel Core i5-7200**U**
> Intel Core i5-<u>7300</u>**HQ**

Also the higher the number after 'i5', eg 7300, the better the performance.

Intel Core i7. The successor to the Core i5.

Intel Core i9. The successor to the Core i7

AMD Ryzen Series. High powered chips from AMD designed to compete with Intel Core i series. Great alternative to Intel chips and good for gaming and high powered laptops.

For example: AMD 8-Core **Ryzen R7** 1700.

Memory (RAM)

Main memory, also called RAM, or primary storage is where the computer loads apps or programs you are currently using. When you open an app or file, it is loaded off the hard disk drive into main memory (RAM), where you can use the app or work on the file.

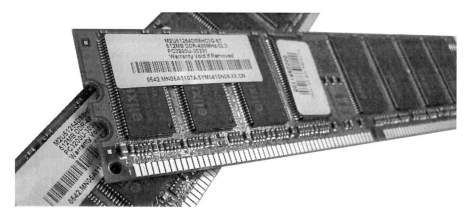

You might have 8 or 16GB of RAM on your computer. Some higher end machines might have more.

Hard Disk

The hard disk, also known as a hard drive, or secondary storage, is where the computer permanently stores all your files and software currently installed on the computer. Sometimes this is incorrectly referred to as the computer's memory which is misleading, as  it is often confused with main memory (RAM). These are two different components. The main memory or RAM is where programs and files are loaded for you to work on, and is a bit like your work desk. The hard disk is where programs are and files are permanently stored, much like a filing cabinet.

When you start up an application such as Microsoft word, the Microsoft word software is loaded up off the hard disk into the computer's main memory (RAM), where you can work on your documents.

There are two types of hard disk - the traditional hard disk shown above simply known as a hard disk drive, and a new type called a solid state drive. These drives perform much like a traditional Hard Disk but are extremely fast and also expensive. They have no moving parts and are composed of flash memory, which is a type of memory that retains data even if the power is turned off.

Motherboard

All the components connect to a large circuit board called a motherboard and is the main circuit board found in desktop and laptop computer systems. It holds many of the crucial components, such as the processor (or CPU) and memory (or RAM), and provides connectors for other peripherals.

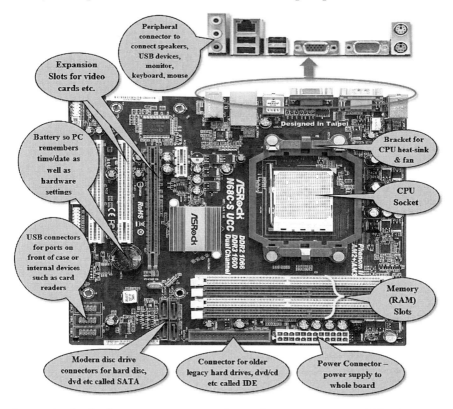

A typical desktop computer has its processor (CPU), main memory (RAM), and other essential components connected to the motherboard. Other components such as storage (hard disc, dvd drive) can be connected to the drive connectors on the motherboard using cables, as can be seen in the photograph opposite.

Cards for video display and sound may be attached to the motherboard, and plug into the expansion slots. In modern computers it is increasingly common to integrate some of these devices into the motherboard itself namely video and sound cards.

Expansion Slots

Video cards and sound cards plug into expansion slots on your motherboard. On modern motherboards, the expansion slots are called PCI express (PCIe) - a high-speed serial expansion bus.

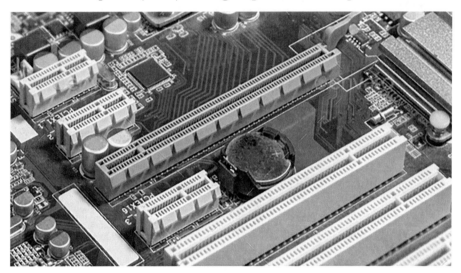

The 'PCIe x 1' slots are for smaller devices such as add on sound, ethernet and wifi network cards etc.

The 'PCIe x 16' slots are extremely fast and are for high end graphics cards like the one in the previous section.

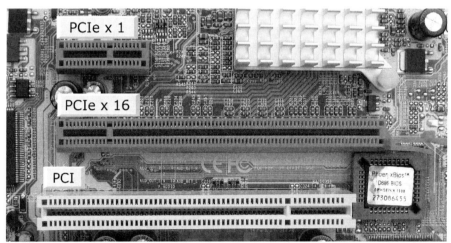

Older PCI slots are still found on some motherboards but are now obsolete.

Sound Card

A sound card, also known as an audio card, is an internal expansion card that facilitates the input and output of audio signals to and from a computer. This allows multimedia applications such as music, video, audio, presentations, and games to play sound through a speaker or sound system.

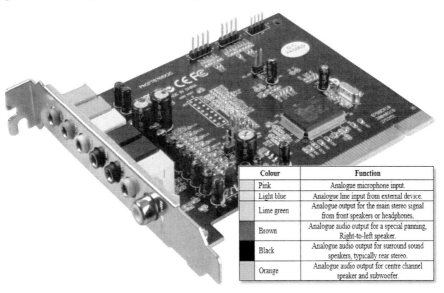

Colour	Function
Pink	Analogue microphone input.
Light blue	Analogue line input from external device.
Lime green	Analogue output for the main stereo signal from front speakers or headphones.
Brown	Analogue audio output for a special panning, Right-to-left speaker.
Black	Analogue audio output for surround sound speakers, typically rear stereo.
Orange	Analogue audio output for centre channel speaker and subwoofer.

Sound cards are usually integrated into most modern motherboards, using basically the same components as a plug-in card.

The best plug-in cards, which use better and more expensive components, can achieve higher quality than integrated sound and are usually used in higher end applications such as audio production, music composition and video editing. Some sound cards have more specialist connections such as digital output for connecting to sound systems and amplifiers.

Some sound cards are external and connect using USB. These are useful if you're using a laptop and allow you to connect various audio devices to your machine.

25

Video Card

The video card or graphics card is responsible for processing video, graphic and visual effects you see on your monitor. The graphics card is also known as a GPU (graphics processing unit).

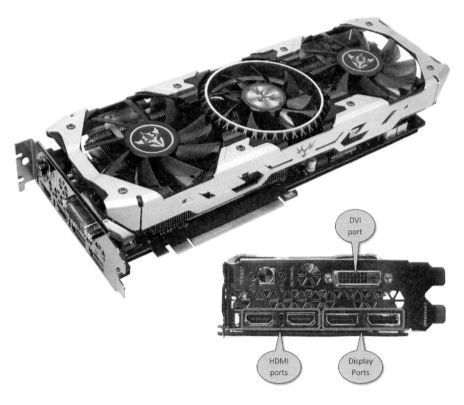

Most video cards offer various functions such as accelerated rendering of 3D scenes and 2D graphics, MPEG-2/MPEG-4 decoding, TV output, or the ability to connect multiple monitors.

Most modern motherboards have video cards integrated into them, eliminating the need for a plug-in card. However, integrated video cards are not usually as high quality as plug in cards. This makes plug in cards more suited to high end video production, graphics processing and video games.

Some plug in video cards have more specialist connections such as HDMI, DVI, S-Video or Composite for connecting to high end televisions, projectors and monitors.

An example of a graphics card is the GeForce GTX 1080 Ti.

Screens

Screens come in different sizes. For laptops the average screen size is 15 inches.

Remember, you measure the screen size from corner to corner. This particular laptop has a 15.6" screen.

For desktops, you can get screens in various sizes such as 21 inch to 28 inch and sometimes even bigger.

Resolution

Resolution is the number of pixels that can be displayed. HD has a resolution of 1920 pixels wide, and 1080 pixels high. The more pixels you have the higher the resolution of the screen.

The monitor below is 1280 by 720

Decoding the Jargon

In this section, we'll take a look at come common computer and peripheral specifications you might find online or when shopping for a computer.

Computer Specs

It's worth knowing a bit about these terms before going to the computer store. Here's a typical computer specification:

OVERVIEW	
Type	Laptop
Operating system	Windows 10 (64-bit)

PERFORMANCE	
Processor	- AMD Ryzen 5 4500U Processor
	- Hexa-core
	- 2.3 GHz / 4 GHz
	- 8 MB cache
RAM	8 GB DDR4 (3200 MHz)
Storage	512 GB SSD

SCREEN	
Touchscreen	Yes
Screen size	15.6"
Screen type	IPS LCD
Resolution	Full HD 1920 x 1080p
Screen features	250 nits

CONNECTIVITY	
WiFi	- WiFi 5
Ethernet	No
Bluetooth	Bluetooth 4.2
USB	- USB Type-C x 1
	- USB 2.0 x 2
Video connections	HDMI x 1
Audio connections	3.5 mm jack

SOUND	
Audio software	Bang & Olufson
Speakers	HP dual speakers

The main components to look for are the processor, hard disk storage, and RAM. In any case, the higher the numbers the better. SSDs are Solid State Drives and are a lot faster than traditional mechanical Hard Disk Drives (HDD).

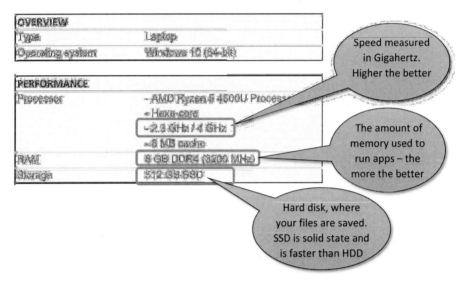

For laptops, screen size is important, but depends on your needs. A larger laptop would be more difficult to carry around but a smaller screen might be more difficult to work with. 15 inch is usually a good size with a resolution of 1920 by 1080.

SCREEN	
Touchscreen	Yes
Screen size	15.6"
Screen type	IPS LCD
Resolution	Full HD 1920 x 1080p
Screen features	250 nits

The graphics or video card is also important. If you are only using your computer for browsing the web or typing a few letters, video performance doesn't really matter. However, if you're into video editing, playing games, or using demanding software, then the video card matters. If you see the term 'nit', this is a measure luminance - the higher number the brighter display.

Also, some laptops have touchscreens. These are not a lot of use in normal operation but can be useful for using graphics or artistic apps for drawing, as well as note taking using a pen.

Most modern machines come with a WiFi connection as well bluetooth. USB comes in two types, there is the older USB 2 and 3 which use the square connector, and a newer USB C which uses a smaller rounded connector. If you plan on using your computer to connect to an external monitor or projector, check which video connection it uses - some use HDMI, others use DVI or VGA.

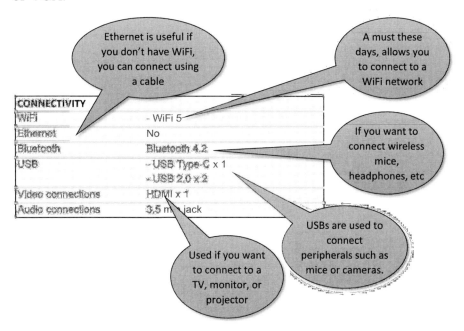

Some other considerations. Sound and speaker systems on laptops are usually poor, so make sure you have at least a 3.5mm audio jack where you can plug in better speakers or headphones.

MEDIA	
Disc drive	No
Memory card reader	2-in-1

FEATURES	
Camera	HP Wide Vision HD camera
Mouse / trackpad	Multi-touch trackpad with gesture
Keyboard	Membrane keyboard

Most laptops and PCs don't come with disc drives anymore - DVD or CD. Also memory card readers are useful if you use a digital camera.

Peripherals

Peripherals are components that connect to a computer. These can be external such as a keyboard, mouse, printer or screen. Or they can be internal such as a graphics card, WiFi card, or disk drive.

In this section, we'll take a look at common peripherals, how they work, and how to install them.

We'll also take a look at some of the most common cables and connectors such as USB, Ethernet, VGA, HDMI and so on.

Printers Types

Printers come in two main types: inkjet and laser.

Inkjet Printer

These printers are good for the average user who just wants to print some letters or other documents and the odd few photographs. They are generally slower printers and are not suitable for printing documents with a large number of pages.

These printers can also print on labels, envelopes and specialist presentation paper (good for greetings cards if you want to print your own).

The only issue I find with inkjet printers is the ink tends to dry up if you don't print out regularly. So make sure you print out something at least once a week to keep the ink from drying up.

Inkjet printers work by forcing tiny droplets of ink in a pattern to form an image.

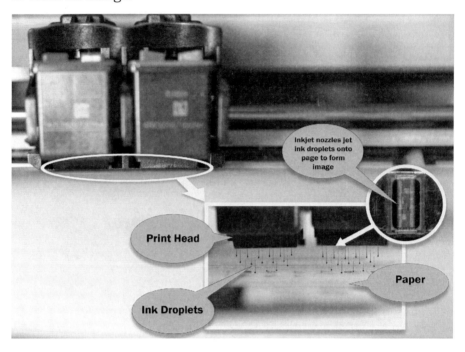

Laser Printer

Laser printers produce high quality prints very quickly and are suited to high volumes of printouts. These printers are good if you do a lot of printing, for example, if you run a business or have a family that all want to print out from their own computers/ laptops at the same time.

These printers print can in black and white or colour and work by burning ink (called toner) onto the page. The toner cartridges are expensive to buy but last a lot longer than ink jet cartridges.

Laser printers use a laser beam to create the image to be printed on an electro-statically charged rotating drum. A corona wire gives the drum a positive static charge.

The laser imprints the image onto the drum using a negative electrical charge.

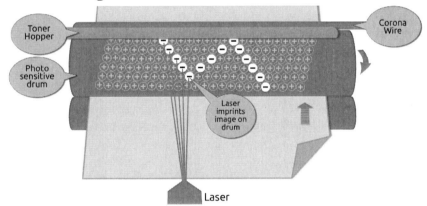

Toner particles being positively charged are attracted to the negatively charged areas of the drum, creating a very sharp image.

The drum then transfers this image onto the paper by direct contact as the paper passes over it.

Finally the image is fused to the paper by the fuser unit, which heats the paper melting the toner and presses it onto the page.

A colour laser printer will go through this process for each of the three primary colours (cyan, magenta, yellow) and black to create a colour image on the page.

Installing Printers

Over the years, printer manufacturers have attempted to make printer setup easier. Most modern printers connect using WiFi.

Printers usually include an app you can use to help you set up your printer. Lets take a look at some common ones.

HP Printers

HP have introduced a simplified setup method for their printers. To set up your printer, plug it in and turn it on. It also helps if your computer is next to your printer.

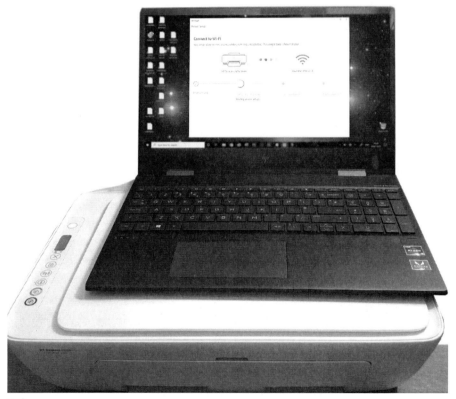

On your computer open your web browser and navigate to the following website

`123.hp.com`

Type your printer's model number into the search field.

Click 'install' or 'get the app'. The app will open in the Microsoft Store, select it, then click 'install'.

If the app doesn't auto launch, start it from the start menu Not all the apps are the same, so they may look different to the images below, but they are similar. Follow the instructions on the screen to download and install the drivers or the app.

Select the option to set up a new printer, then follow the instructions on the screen.

The app will scan for your printer. Click 'set up', then follow the instructions on the screen.

If you want to connect to your printer using Wi-Fi, make sure the printer is on and click **Refresh**. To set up a printer not listed, click **Set up a New Printer**.

HP DeskJet 2600 series

Set Up

Enter your WiFi network name and password. You'll usually find these on the back of your WiFi router.

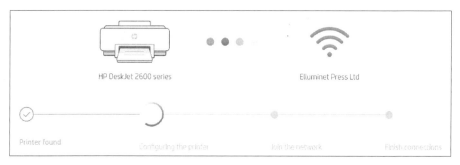

HP DeskJet 2600 series   Elluminet Press Ltd

Printer found   Configuring the printer   Join the network   Finish connections

In some cases, you'll need to add your printer to windows 10. See page 40.

Epson Printers

To set up your printer, plug it in and turn it on. On your computer open your web browser and navigate to the following website

`epson.sn`

Type your printer's model number into the search field.

Setting Up Your Product

Enter the name of your product or select it from all products. e.g. XP-225

XP-225

Product Name

Click 'lets get started'. Scroll down the page. Follow the instructions on the screen to download and install the drivers or the app.

Canon Printers

To set up your printer, plug it in and turn it on. On your computer open your web browser and navigate to the following website

`canon.com/ijsetup`

Click 'setup', then type in your printer model number.

Follow the instructions on the screen to download and install the drivers or the app.

Brother Printers

To set up your printer, plug it in and turn it on. On your computer open your web browser and navigate to the following website

`support.brother.com`

Select 'downloads'.

Type in your model number.

Select 'windows 10', then download the 'full driver & software package'. Follow the instructions on screen.

Add Printer to Windows 10

Your printer will let you know when it's connected to your WiFi - the WiFi light usually stops flashing and lights up. Once connected, on your computer open the settings app from the start menu.

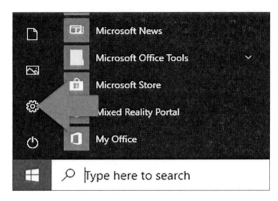

From the settings app, click 'devices'.

Select 'printers & scanners' from the panel on the left hand side, then click 'add a printer or scanner'.

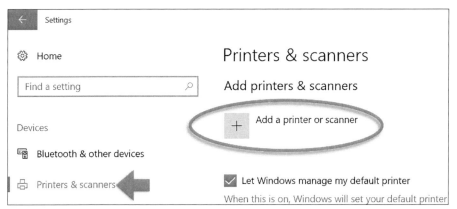

Windows will detect most modern printers. Select your printer from the list.

Select your printer from the list, then click 'add device'.

Windows will download and install the appropriate driver for your printer automatically. If this doesn't work, try downloading the driver for your printer - see page 46.

If you're Struggling to Connect your Printer

If your printer wont connect to your WiFi, there are a few other options you could try.

WPS

If your printer doesn't have an LCD panel, use the WPS method. You can use this method if you have a WPS button on your router

Refer to the printer's quick start guide to find the exact procedure for your printer model. Usually you have to press and hold the WiFi button on your printer for a few seconds, then go to your router and press the WPS button.

If your router doesn't have a WPS button, you'll have to select your WiFi network (SSID) and enter your WiFi password on your printer. You'll need to refer to the printer's instructions on exactly how to do that on your particular printer.

Enter WiFi Network on LCD Panel

Printers with LCD panels display step-by-step instructions for setting up the wireless connection when you first turn on the printer. Each printer is different, so read the instructions for specifics on how to do this.

If you're stuck, try going to the settings section on the LCD panel. This is usually called 'settings', 'setup', or 'preferences'. There might even be a WiFi icon.

Find the network settings. There might be an option for a Wireless Setup Wizard. Select this and run through the prompts.

You need to select your WiFi network name - the name is usually printed on the back of your router. Enter the WiFi password when prompted.

Older Printers

If Windows doesn't detect your printer or you have an older model, click 'the printer I want isn't listed.'

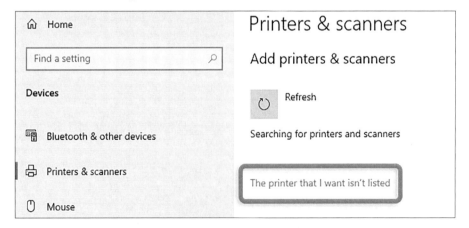

For printers connected via USB select 'my printer is a little older, help me find it.'

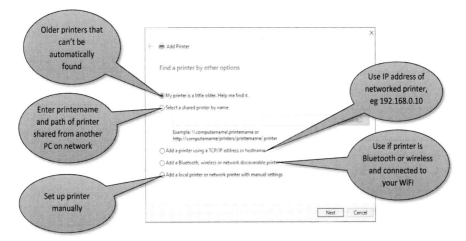

Select your printer from the results list, click 'next',

then give the printer a name if required, click 'next'.

For some of the older printers, Windows may prompt you for driver software. If this is the case cancel the procedure and go to "Downloading Printer Drivers" on page 46.

Select 'do not share this printer' then click next.

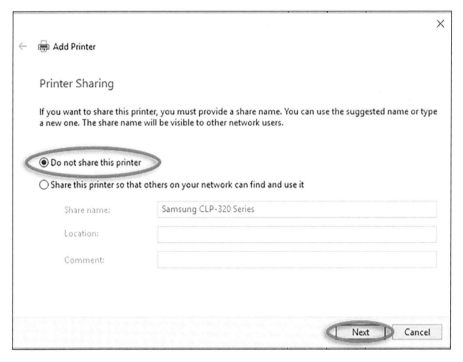

Once you're done, click 'finish'.

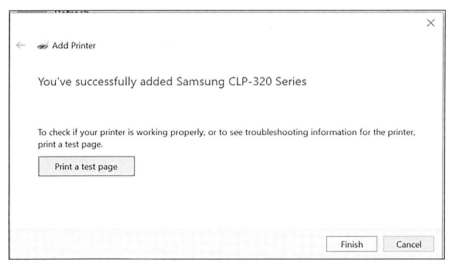

Connect using USB

Using a USB cable, plug the square end into the back of the printer, then plug the other end into a USB port on your computer.

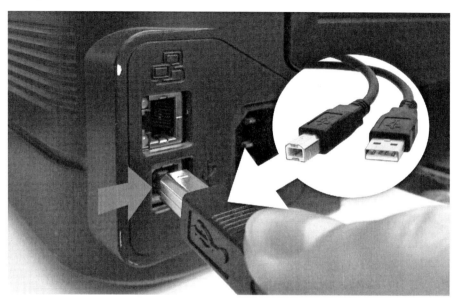

Connect Using Ethernet

Using an ethernet cable, plug one end into the back of the printer, then plug the other end into a port on your router.

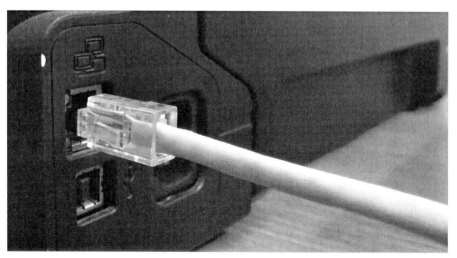

Download the Printer Drivers

If Windows 10 has trouble installing your printer, you'll need to download and install the printer software.

To do this, you'll need to go to the manufacturer's website and download the software.

For HP & Samsung printers go to

`support.hp.com/drivers`

For Canon printers go to

`www.usa.canon.com/support`

For Brother printers go to

`support.brother.com`

For Epson printers go to

`support.epson.com`

Somewhere on the manufacturer's website, there will be a product search field. Type in the model name of your printer. Click 'OK' or 'find'

In the example above, I'm installing an HP printer. In most cases you'll need to download the driver software from the manufacturer's website.

From the search results, select your Operating System if required, usually "Windows 10 (64bit)".

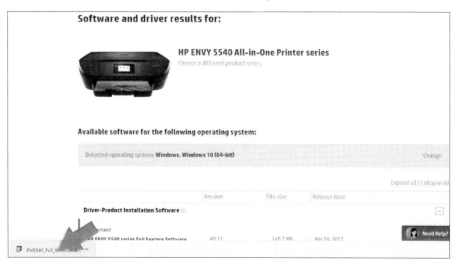

Click on the prompt at the bottom of your browser.

This will run the installation software. Click 'OK' or 'Yes' to the security prompt. If you don't see a prompt, go to your downloads folder in file explorer and double click on the EXE file you just downloaded. Follow the on screen instructions to connect to your printer.

Managing Printers

You can get to the print queue from the Settings App on the start menu. From the Settings App, click 'devices'.

On the left hand side of the window, click 'printers & scanners', then select your printer. From the options that open up, click 'open queue'.

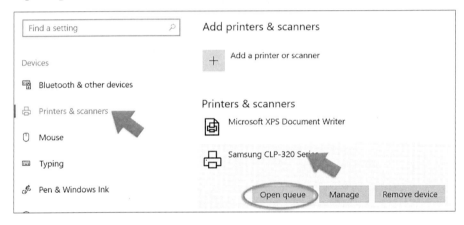

This will open up the print queue for that printer.

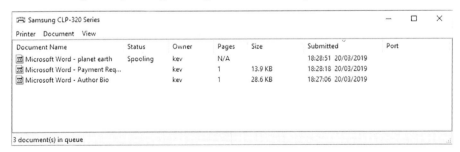

Here you can see a list of documents that are queued for printing. If you right click on the print job in the list, you can cancel or pause the document. You can also change global printer settings and preferences here too.

Print Problems

With inkjet printers, poor print quality prints are often caused by blocked print heads or where the ink has dried. This is common on inkjet printers, especially if you haven't printed anything for a while. To clean the print heads, find the printer software that was installed on your computer when you set up the printer. This is usually in a folder on the start menu. It's difficult to give specifics here as different manufactures have different software. With HP printers its usually an app. Launch the printer app. Find the 'maintenance' section, 'tools', or 'quality tools'.

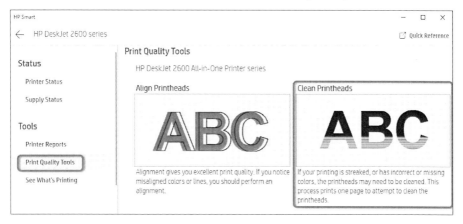

Select 'clean print heads'. You may need to do this several times.

With Epson, Canon, and Brother, open your settings app, select devices, then click 'printers & scanners'. Select your printer, click 'open queue'. Go to 'printer' menu, select 'printing preferences'.

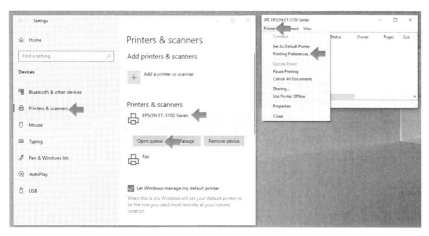

Once the software opens, find the maintenance, settings, or tools section. Run the head cleaning program.

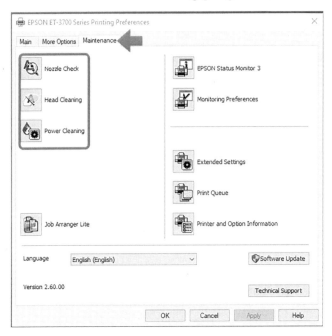

If your printer won't print, check the connections. Make sure it is connected to your computer either over WiFi, USB or ethernet. Open the printer app and check your printer is online

Mouse

Computer mice come in various different shapes, however most of them have two click buttons and a scroll wheel. Some have other buttons you can assign various functions to. You'll want to find a mouse that fits comfortably in your hand allowing you to use both buttons and the scroll wheel without straining your wrist. Mice can be wired or wireless. Wireless mice are nice to use as they don't have a wire hanging out the side which can get in the way. These mice either need batteries or recharged.

Adjustments

You should also adjust the pointer speed to your own preference. To change the speed. Open your settings app, select devices, then select 'mouse' from the list on the left.

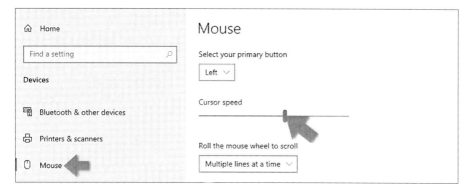

Set the speed fast enough so the mouse pointer moves across the screen without you having to move your wrist or arm too much.

Using the Mouse

When using your mouse, make sure it fits securely into the palm of your hand. This will allow you to use both mouse buttons comfortably and reduce wrist strain. When you move the mouse, try keep wrist movement to a minimum.

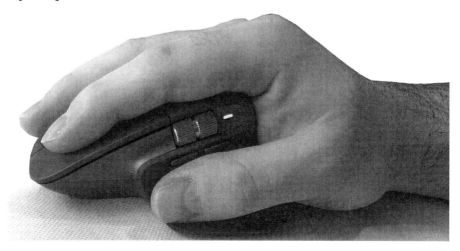

Move the mouse along your desk, while keeping an eye on the mouse pointer on the screen.

Left Click

The most common function of your mouse is the left click. This is used to select something on the screen. You can select an icon, file, button, or text field. Move your mouse pointer to the object on the screen, then click once with the left mouse button.

Double Click

To start an app, application, or open a file, you need to double click. This means clicking the left mouse button twice in quick succession.

Right Click

The right mouse button opens a context menu on an object such as a file or app. This provides in context functionality for that file or app.

Here, in the screen on the right, you'll see I've right clicked on a file in File Explorer. This brings up the context menu with additional functions you can perform on that file.

Scroll Wheel

The scroll wheel allows you to scroll up and down pages in a document, a window such as File Explorer, or a web page in Chrome or Edge. Move your mouse pointer over the page you want to scroll, use your index finger to move the wheel up or down.

Touch Pad

The touchpad is usually found on laptop devices and allows you to control the mouse pointer using your finger.

You can also scroll, zoom and right click using various gestures.

Left Click on Something

Use one finger to tap on the touch pad. Slide left, right, up, down to move the mouse pointer on screen. Tap on the touch pad to select something, double tap to open an app or file.

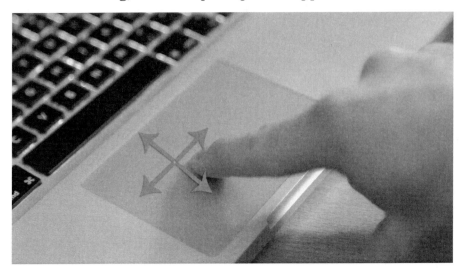

Right Click on Something

To right click on something - to open a popup menu, move the mouse pointer to an icon, then tap with two fingers.

Scroll

Use two fingers up and down the touch pad to scroll up and down web pages, documents or emails.

Keyboards

Computer keyboards come with the standard QWERTY layout. There are other layouts for other regions and languages but we'll concentrate on the QWERTY design. Here is a common example

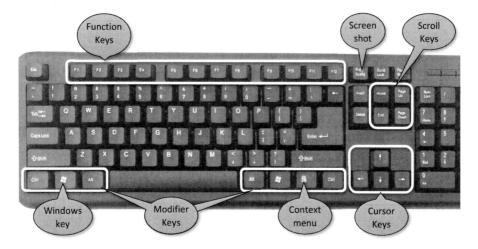

Function Keys

Along the top of the keyboard you'll see some function keys. These arc usually assigned a standard function within windows.

Lets take a look at what each key does.

Key	Function
F1	Used to access the help screen
F2	Renames a selected icon, folder or file
F3	Often opens a search
F4	Open the address bar in file explorer
F5	Refresh document, page or window
F6	Jumps to address bar in browser
F7	Spell/grammar check in Word
F8	
F9	Refreshes a document in Word or sends and receives emails in Outlook
F10	Activates the menu bar of an open application.
F11	Full screen mode
F12	Save as in most windows programs. Also opens developer tools in web browser

Modifier Keys

Modifier keys are used when executing a keyboard short cut, such as CTRL C to copy text. CTRL, or control is the modifier key. Here are some useful keyboard shortcuts.

Windows + Tab	Opens thumbnail list of open applications
Windows + A	Open Windows 10 notification centre
Windows + D	Show Windows desktop
Windows + E	Open Windows Explorer
Windows + K	Connect to wireless displays and audio devices
Windows + P	Project a screen
Windows + R	Run a command
Windows + X	Open Start button context menu
Windows key + Arrow key	Snap app windows left, right, corners, maximize, or minimize
Windows key + Comma	Temporarily peek at the desktop
Windows Key	Show windows start menu
Alt + Tab	Switch to previous window
Alt + Space	Reveals drop down menu on current window: Restore, move, size, minimize, maximize or close.
Alt + F4	Close current app
Ctrl + Shift + Esc	Open Task Manager
Ctrl + Z	Undo Command
Ctrl + X	Cut selected text
Ctrl + C	Copy selected text
Ctrl + V	Paste selected text at cursor position
Ctrl + P	Print

Some keyboard will have special keys on the right hand side such as insert or home, page up and page down. 'Home' moves the cursor to the beginning of the line, 'end' moves it to the end. You can use these when typing a document as they help when moving around the page.

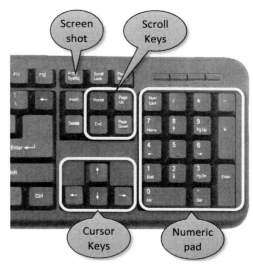

Below that, you'll see some cursor keys. These are useful when moving up and down a page, or moving your cursor around a word document.

On the far right you'll see a numeric pad. These keys are useful if you work with numbers as the keypad makes it easier and faster to enter numbers.

Flash Drives & External Drives

You can attach storage devices to your computer. The most common ones are memory sticks - also called usb keys, usb sticks, flash drives or thumb drives. The other type is the portable hard drive.

Memory sticks are usually smaller in capacity ranging from 1GB all the way up to 256GB. Portable hard drives can be larger than 1TB.

To read the drive, plug the device into a USB port on your computer, then select file explorer from the task bar.

The device will show up in File Explorer, under 'This PC' section.

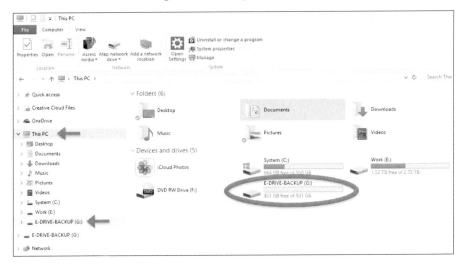

Double click the drive icon, circled above, to open the contents of the drive.

To copy files to the drive, just drag and drop them from file explorer. To do this, select the folder from the left hand side of file explorer, where the files you want to copy are saved - this could be on OneDrive or 'This PC'. In this example, I'm copying a file from the 'documents' folder in the 'this pc' section.

From the pane on the right hand side, click and drag the file you want to the external drive, as shown below.

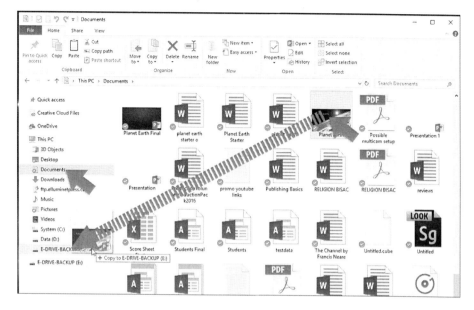

External DVD Drive

A somewhat dying breed nowadays but CD and DVD drives are still available. Many laptops and PCs no longer include these and if they don't, you can buy an external USB DVD drive like the one below. The device plugs into a USB port on your computer and shows up in File Explorer as another Drive.

You can play your favourite movies, CDs if you still have them on disk. If you want to play a DVD, you'll need to download some software first.

Just go to the following website and download the software.

`www.videolan.org`

Click the 'Download VLC' on the homepage.

Click 'Run' when prompted by your browser and follow the instructions on screen.

You'll find the program on your start menu in the 'video lan' folder. click 'VLC Media Player'

Click the play button on the bottom left of the VLC Media Player window.

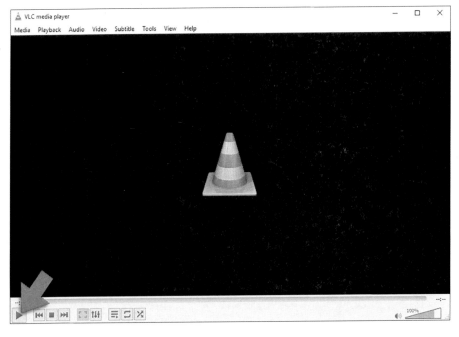

NAS Drives

NAS drives, sometimes called Network Attached Storage, allow you to store and backup files to a central point on a network.

All the machines on the network can access files on the NAS drive. Shared data can either be set to private for one particular machine or shared publicly for all machines to see.

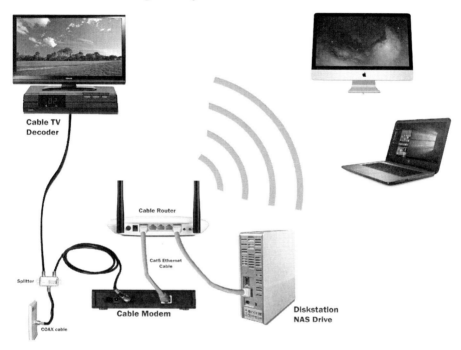

These devices make great backup strategies and come with software you can install on your computer to automate backups at certain times. You will need a few terabytes of storage on your NAS.

To connect to a shared folder, you'll need to enter the UNC path to that folder. The UNC path is the name of the NAS sharing the folder, followed by the folder name.

`\\NAS-Name\Shared-Folder-Name`

Type the UNC path to the shared folder into the address bar along the top of the window. In this case:

`\\diskstation\documents`

Other Peripherals

Other peripherals include scanners, cameras, game control pads, virtual reality headsets, and so on.

Most external peripherals connect to the computer through a data port using a USB cable. Some older peripherals connect using firewire, but most use USB. eSATA ports can connect certain external hard drives. The SPDIF port is an optical audio port that allows you to connect high end sound systems.

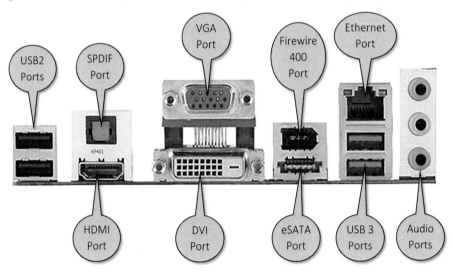

Monitors, projectors and other screens are connected using either HDMI, VGA or DVI.

3.5mm phono jacks are used to connect microphones and speaker systems to a computer. The blue port is called 'line in' and is used to connect external audio devices for recording. The green port is called 'line out' and is used to connect speaker systems and headphones. The pink port is called 'mic in' and is used to connect microphones.

Data Ports

Data ports allow you to connect devices to your computer. The most common data ports are USB, Ethernet.

USB

USB stands for Universal Serial Bus and is a universal connection used to connect all different types of peripherals to your computer as easy as possible using the same connection type.

USB 3.0, shown below left, was released on 12 November 2008, with a data rate of around 4 Gbps and is much faster than USB 2.0.

USB 2.0, shown below right, was released in April 2000, with a maximum data rate of 480 Mbps.

USB 3.0 ports are colour coded in blue, while USB 2.0 ports are colour coded in black.

The smaller USB pictured below left is called micro USB and the one next to it is called mini USB.

USB-C

USB C is a newer USB standard with a data rate between 10 & 20 Gbps and is much faster than USB 3.0.

The USB C port is different than the previous two and looks like this:

The USB C plug is a double sided connector meaning it can be plugged into a USB C port either way up.

Many new tablets and phones are now starting to include the USB-C port.

Some of the newer laptops are also including USB-C ports.

Ethernet

Also known as RJ45, Ethernet is used to connect a computer or laptop to a network and to the internet.

FireWire

Also known as IEEE 1394 or iLink, this port was widely used in digital camcorders and most of them that recorded onto tape included a firewire interface .

There were two versions; Firewire 400 (on the left) and Firewire 800 (on the right).

FireWire 400 transfers data at about 400Mbps, Firewire 800 transfers data at about 800Mbps

ThunderBolt

Thunderbolt ports are used for peripherals that require extremely fast data transfers and have been known to support speeds of up to 10Gbps.

This port is also used on Apple Mac computers as a mini display port for connecting to monitors and projectors.

eSATA

eSATA cables connect to some types of high speed external portable hard drives. The eSATA cable cannot transmit power, unless you use eSATAp (powered eSATA).

Video Ports

Monitors/computer screens and projectors connect to your PC or laptop using a variety of different connectors.

Many tablets and smaller computers have micro versions of these ports, eg micro USB or micro HDMI

DVI

Digital Video Interface is a video display interface used to connect a video source (eg your computer) to a display device, such as an HD ready TV, computer monitor or projector.

DVI can get a bit confusing, as there are a number of different connectors. Here is a summary.

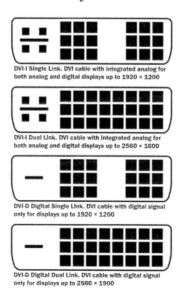

DVI-I Single Link. DVI cable with integrated analog for both analog and digital displays up to 1920 × 1200

DVI-I Dual Link. DVI cable with integrated analog for both analog and digital displays up to 2560 × 1600

DVI-D Digital Single Link. DVI cable with digital signal only for displays up to 1920 × 1200

DVI-D Digital Dual Link. DVI cable with digital signal only for displays up to 2560 × 1900

HDMI

High Definition Media Interface, is a combined audio/video interface for carrying video and audio data from a High Definition device such as a games console or computer to a high end computer monitor, video projector, or High Definition digital television.

Pictured below is Standard HDMI & Micro HDMI.

VGA

Video Graphics Array is a 15-pin connector found on many computers and laptops and is used to connect to projectors, computer monitors and LCD television sets.

Component Video

Carries a video signal (no audio) that has been split into three component channels: red, green, blue. It is often used to connect high end dvd players to televisions.

Composite Video

Carries an analogue standard definition video signal combining red, green, blue channels (with no audio) and is used in old games consoles or analogue video cameras.

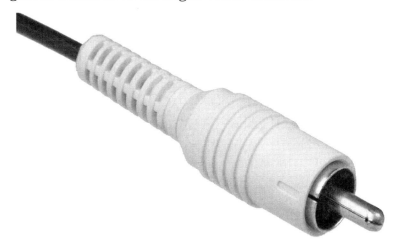

Audio Ports

Audio ports allow you to connect audio devices to your computer such as mics and speakers

1/8" (3.5mm) Phono Jack

The phono jack also known as an audio jack, headphone jack or jack plug, is commonly used to connect speakers or headphones to a computer, laptop, tablet or MP3 player and carries analogue audio signals.

1/4" (6.35mm) Phono Jack

These are generally used on a wide range of professional audio equipment. 6.35 mm (1/4 in) plugs are common on audio recorders, musical instruments such as guitars and amps.

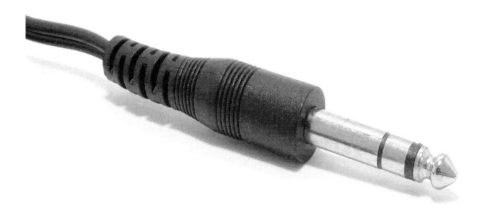

3 Pin XLR

The XLR connector is usually found on professional audio, video, and stage lighting equipment.

Many audio mixing desks have XLR connectors to connect stage mics and instruments.

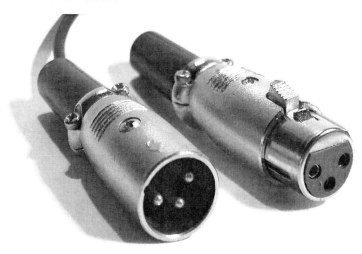

RCA Audio

Some home audio system, televisions and DVD players use RCA cables to connect to audio receivers, amplifiers and speakers.

Computer Software

Without software a computer is pretty much useless. Computer software comes in a variety of different forms: Applications, Apps, Utilities, and System Software.

Applications are pieces of software that are quite large and were originally designed to run on a desktop computer; you interact with the application using a keyboard and mouse. Example applications are: Microsoft Office Suite, Adobe Creative Suite, and so on.

A more recent incarnation of software is the App. Apps are usually smaller in size and are designed with a touch screen in mind. So for example, facebook has an app. Microsoft Office Suite also has App versions of its software to complement their desktop application counterparts.

Utilities are small programs that are designed to configure, analyse, optimise or maintain a computer, such as antivirus, scandisk or defrag.

The most important piece of software is called the Operating System such as Windows 10, MacOS, iOS or Linux. This is called system software.

The Operating System

The Operating System or OS is a piece of system software that manages all the hardware and software resources available on your computer. This could be memory allocation, storage device management, file management, as well as providing a nice user interface of windows and icons for you to interact with.

On laptops, PCs and some tablets you'd have Microsoft Windows 10 as your Operating System.

I will cover the very basics of Windows 10 in this section. For more detailed information on specifics on using Windows 10, check out the other book in the series. Windows 10 Fundamentals. ISBN: 979-8727083581

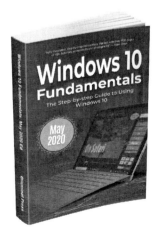

Running Windows the First Time

If you've just bought a new computer with Windows 10, or just installed a fresh copy, you'll need to run through the initial set up procedure.

Regional Settings

Select your country or region from the list and click 'yes'.

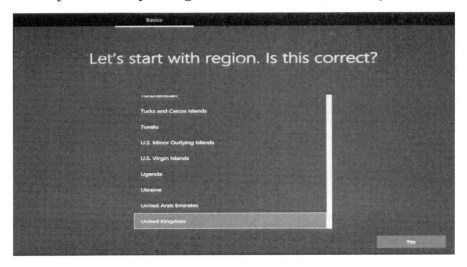

Select keyboard layout for your country, then click 'yes'. Skip secondary keyboard if you don't have one.

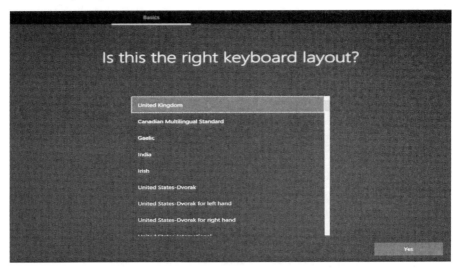

Terms Of Use

On the terms and agreements page click on 'Accept'.

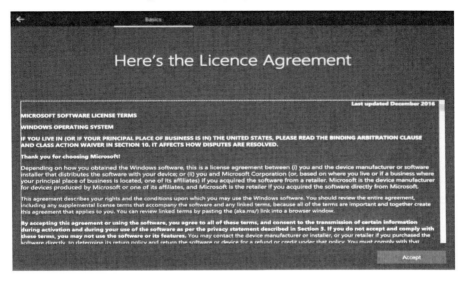

Connect to your WiFi

Select your WiFi network from the list of detected networks. This is usually printed on your router/modem or you can find out from your service provider. Click 'connect' from the box that appears.

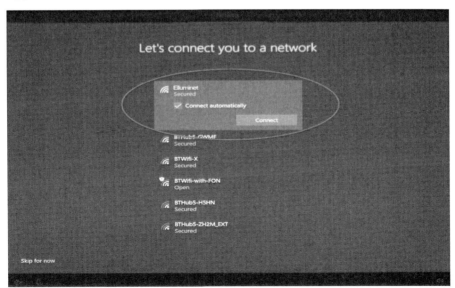

Enter WiFi Password

Enter the password for your WiFi network. This will be printed on the back of your router/modem, or you can find out from your service provider.

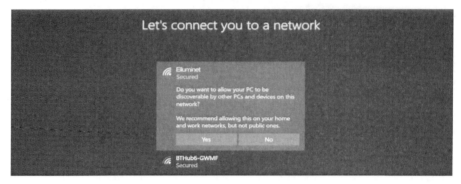

Click 'yes' to the prompt if you are on your home WiFi network. Click 'no' if you're using a public WiFi hotspot such as a library, coffee shop or airport - you don't want other people to see you on a public network.

Sign in for the First Time

Sign in with your Microsoft Account email address and password, then click 'next'. This allows you to make use of OneDrive, email, purchase apps from the App Store, buy music and films.

If you don't have one, click 'create one', and fill in the form.

Set a PIN Code

Click 'Set a PIN code', then tap in your code, if you want the extra security. This means you can enter a 4 digit pin code instead of a password.

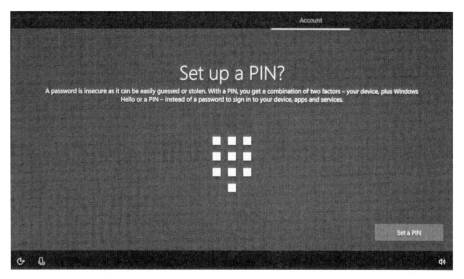

Link your Phone

This allows you access text messages, photos, contacts from your phone, and works best with android devices. Type in your phone number and hit 'send'. Click 'next' to continue.

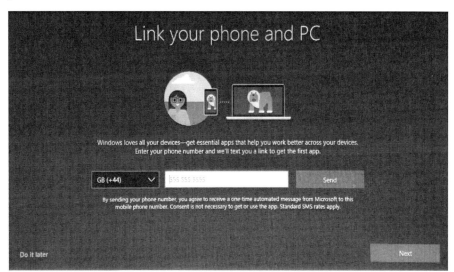

Set up OneDrive

OneDrive is your online storage where you can store your files and access them from any of your devices. Click 'yes' to enable OneDrive.

Meet Cortana

Here you can enable your digital assistant and use voice commands.

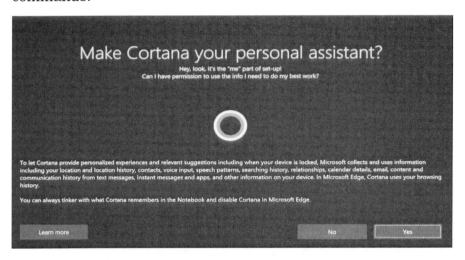

Click 'yes' to enable Cortana, or click 'no' if you can't be bothered talking to your computer.

Do More with your Voice

If you're using Cortana, select 'use speech recognition', this helps Cortana understand you better. Select 'accept'.

Location

This allows windows to determine your physical location. This enables you to use location based apps such as weather, local interest, news as well as maps, and getting directions. To turn it on select 'yes'. If you don't plan on using any of these apps, then turn it off. Select 'accept'.

Find my Device

This is useful if you're setting up a tablet and allows windows to periodically report its location. This can help if you lose your device or it is stolen. You'll be able to see its location in your Microsoft Account settings. Select 'yes', then 'accept'.

Send Diagnostic Data

Diagnostic data is what Microsoft uses to troubleshoot problems and make improvements to its services. I'd suggest you select 'basic', so the only data that is sent to Microsoft is your device settings and its current state of operation, select 'accept'.

Improve Inking & Typing

This is data collected when you use Windows Ink and allows Microsoft to use the data to improve its product. Leaving this feature on is usually ok. Select 'yes' then 'accept'.

Get Tailored Experiences with Diagnostic Data

Allow Windows to tailor your computing experience to your personal tastes. This will give you tips and recommendations based on how you use Windows. To enable this, select 'yes', then 'accept'.

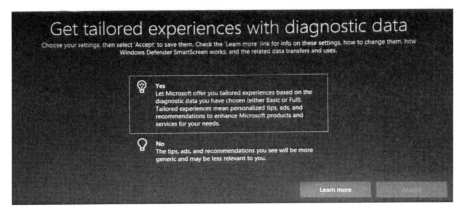

Let Apps use Advertising ID

This means any ads that appear will be tailored to your personal computing habits. Select 'yes', then 'accept'.

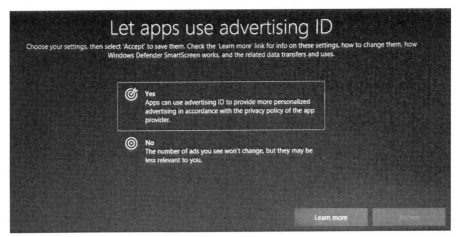

Once Windows has all your preferences and details, it will configure your computer. Time for a coffee... this will take a while.

Once the configuration is complete, you'll land on the Windows 10 desktop.

The Windows Desktop

The desktop is the basic working area on your PC. It's the equivalent of your workbench or office desk, hence why it is called a desktop.

Desktop Anatomy

On the desktop itself you can save files such as documents or photos - these will appear as file icons. On some devices you may see other icons such as the trash can for deleted files or network connections.

Along the bottom of the desktop, you'll find the start button on the left, windows search - to search for files or apps, cortana, as well as pinned and running apps. Over on the right hand side of the task bar you'll see status icons, the clock/calendar, and the action centre.

Start Menu

The start menu is the central launch point for apps, changing settings, as well as system shut down, reset, hibernate, and sleep. To open the start menu, click the start button on the bottom left of the screen.

Lets take a closer look at the different parts of the menu.

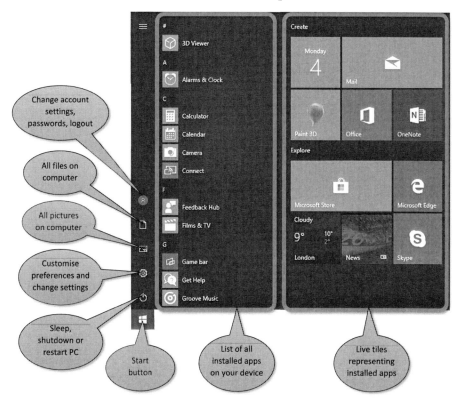

Listed down the far left hand side of your menu you'll see five little icons. From top to bottom, these icons allow you to change your account password or log out, view all files & pictures using file explorer, system settings, and shut down.

Also down the left is a list of your most frequently used applications. Underneath this list is an alphabetical list of all apps installed on your system.

On the right hand side of the menu, you'll see coloured tiles representing apps. This is the tile area and these tiles are sometimes called live tiles.

Live tiles graphically represent apps and can also display basic notifications such as latest messages, or emails from your mail app, information such as weather, latest news headlines and so on, even when the app isn't running. To run the app you just click on the tile.

Task Bar

The taskbar shows which programs are currently running. As you open apps, the app's icons appear along the taskbar with a line underneath indicating that the app is running.

Anatomy

The taskbar also serves as a shortcut bar so you can pin apps you use most often and switch to other apps running in the background.

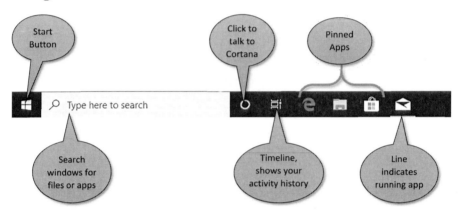

You'll also see the start button, icons for windows search, cortana and your timeline activity history.

On the far right you will see the notification area or status area, sometimes incorrectly called the system tray. This has icons representing battery, WiFi

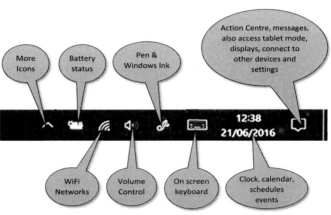

networks, volume control, pen/ink, onscreen keyboard, clock, and action center. Click on these icons to view their details. Eg, click on the clock to view your calendar and upcoming events, or click on the volume control to adjust your audio volume.

System Icons

Over on the right hand side of the taskbar you'll see your system icons in the system area. The icons that appear here will depend on what device you're using and what apps you have installed.

With these icons, you can adjust the volume using the audio icon, connect to WiFi using the WiFi icon, open OneDrive settings and so on. Some of the icons will be hidden, to reveal all the icons, click the small up arrow on the far left of the system icons.

Action Centre

The action centre shows alerts and messages from different applications, as well as some shortcut controls. To open action center, click the notifications icon on the bottom right of the screen. If you're using a touch screen, swipe inwards from the right edge of the screen.

At the top of action center, you'll see notifications and messages. These could be email message that have just arrived, system messages or status alerts from applications.

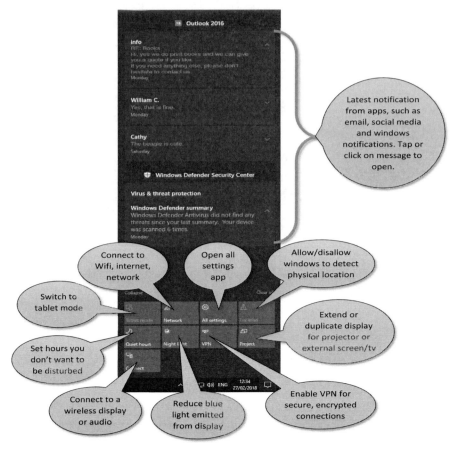

Along the bottom of the notifications window you will see your 'quick actions' such as tablet mode, display settings, media connect for connecting to projectors, second screens etc. Click on these to adjust the settings. Click 'expand' if you don't see all of the icons.

Timeline Activity History

You'll find the timeline icon on your task bar on the bottom left of your screen, next to Windows search and Cortana. Click the icon to open timeline.

When timeline opens, you'll see a history of apps, websites and files you've used, organised in reverse chronological order.

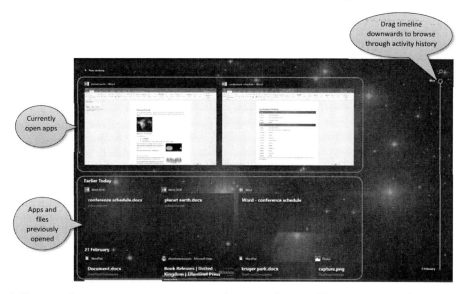

Files and apps you are currently running, will appear at the top. You can click or tap on these to switch to them.

Along the right hand side you'll see the timeline. You can drag this down to browse through your activity history.

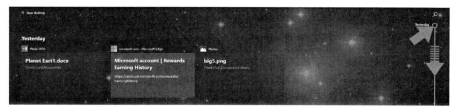

You'll see apps and files you've had open listed according to the date you last used them. Click or tap on any of these files to go back to where you left off.

On the top right of the screen, you'll see a magnifying glass.

This allows you to search for activities, files you've used and so on. Type the name of the file in the search field. Click any of the documents in the search results to open them up.

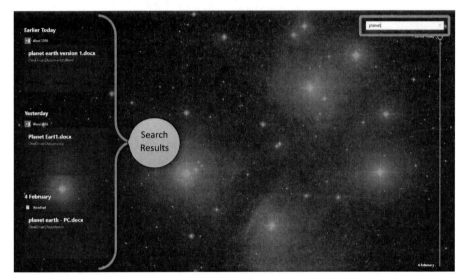

To remove an activity, right click on the thumbnail preview of the activity you want to delete, then select 'remove'.

To clear all the history for a particular day, select 'clear all...' from the popup menu.

Windows Search

Windows search has now been separated from Cortana. You'll find the search field on the bottom left of the taskbar.

With Windows search you can search for files, apps, email, music, people, and settings on your PC, as well as a web search. To do this, click in the search field on the bottom left of your taskbar.

When the search window opens, you'll see media you can search for along the top: apps, documents, email, web, more. This is useful if you want to search only for documents, email, or apps, rather than your whole PC. This helps to narrow down your search.

Underneath, you'll see icons representing the most used apps on your PC. These could be anything such Microsoft Word, File Explorer, or even your favourite games. Windows keeps track of the applications you use and displays them here. Click the icons to open the apps. Further down the window, you'll see your most recently opened files, emails, and websites. Click a file or website in the list to open it.

Searching for Files

To search for something, type it into the search field on the taskbar. This could be the name of an app, a document, email, or website.

Chapter 3: Computer Software

On the left hand side of the search results, you'll see a list of files, apps, and web search suggestions.

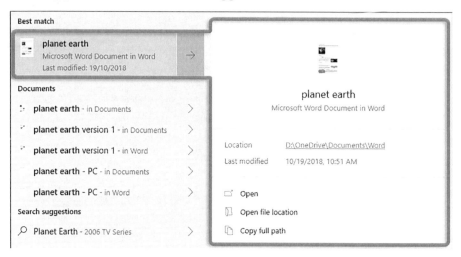

Press the down arrow key on your keyboard to scroll down the list to see some details about the search result. These details will appear in the right hand half of the window. Click on the search suggestion in the list on the left hand side to open it up.

Searching for Apps

You can also search for apps, just type the name of the app into the search field on the bottom left of the taskbar. Click the app to open it.

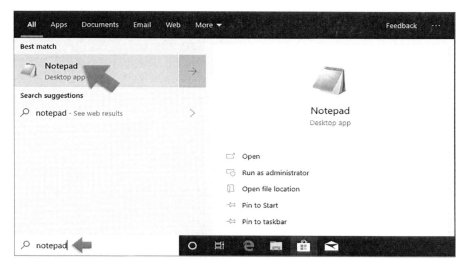

Searching for Windows Settings

You can also search for settings. For example, you can search for printer settings, WiFi, BlueTooth, display settings and so on. Just type the setting you're looking for into the search field on the bottom left of the taskbar. Click the setting you want to open it up.

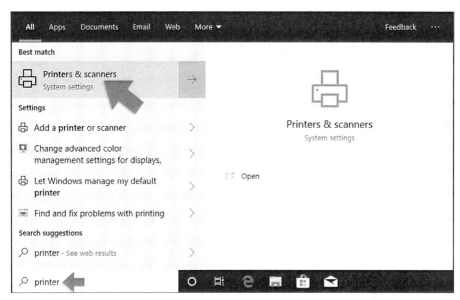

Narrowing Down the Search

Along the top of the window, you'll see a bar with some options. These allow you to restrict your search to apps, documents, email, web, folders, music, people, photos, settings, or videos (click 'more' to see the rest of the options).

So, if I was searching for 'planet earth' on the web, I'd select 'web' from the options on the bar. If I just wanted to search my email, I'd select 'email' from the options.

File Explorer

File explorer can be used to find your files on your computer, access your OneDrive, network resources, and external hard drives or flash drives.

You'll find file explorer on your taskbar, or on your start menu.

Down the left hand side of the main window, you will find a list of all the libraries of files on your computer, ie documents, photographs, music and videos, as well as external drives, and network resources.

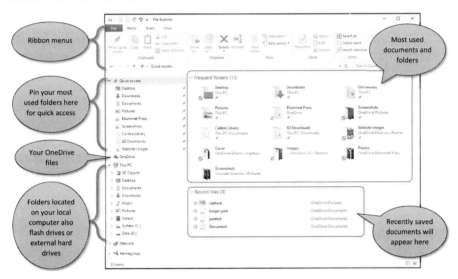

In the right hand pane at the top, Windows will start to list the most used folders you have accessed. If you click on 'quick access' on the top left, you will see a list of your most recently accessed files.

You can select any of the folders in the left hand pane. When you do this, the contents of those folders will appear in the right hand pane.

Along the top of the explorer window you will see the ribbon menus. This is where you'll find tools to create new folders, copy or move files, share files, sort files, and so on. You can select the different ribbons using the tabs along the top of the screen.

Home Ribbon

On the home ribbon, you'll find all your most common tools, such as copy and paste files, create folders, move files, delete files and show file properties.

Share Ribbon

On the share ribbon you can burn files to a CD, print them, zip them up into a compressed file - useful if you want to email a few documents together. Or you can share files with other computers on your home network, email, or near share.

View Ribbon

With the view ribbon you can display your files as a list, as icons and as thumbnails. Icons and thumbnail views can be useful for browsing photographs. To do this click on the layout options in the middle of the ribbon (large icons, medium sized icons, list or details).

Chapter 3: Computer Software

Organising your Files

There are many different types of file types; files for photos, videos, documents, speadsheets, presentations and so on. These files are identified by a file extension.

```
filename.extension
```

So for example...

A photograph is usually saved as a JPEG or JPG. Eg **photo-of-sophie.jpg**. This could be from a graphics package or a camera.

A document is usually saved as a DOC or DOCX. Eg: **production-resume.docx**. This is usually from a word processor such as Microsoft Word.

The 3 or 4 letters after the period is called a file extension and it is what Windows uses to identify the application needed to open the file.

Windows stores your files in a hierarchical tree like structure.

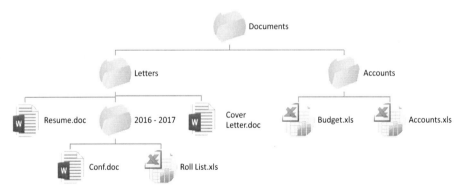

You can create yellow folders to store files of the same type or for the same purpose.

In the example above, letters to various recipients are stored in a 'letters' folder. This can be further divided into year folders, so you have one for each year.

Similarly, all files to do with the accounts are stored in an 'accounts' folder.

Storing files in this fashion keeps them organised and makes them easier to find.

Creating Folders

It's a good idea to create folders to help organise all your files. You could have a folder for your personal documents, work documents, presentations, vacation/holiday photos, college work and so on. To do this open your File Explorer.

On the left hand side of your screen, navigate to the place you want to create a folder. In this example, I'm going to create a folder in my 'OneDrive'.

From the home ribbon along the top of your screen, click 'new folder'.

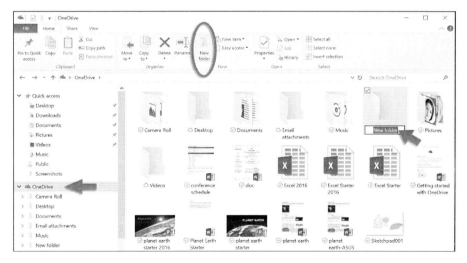

On the right hand side of your screen, you'll see a new folder appear called 'new folder'.

Delete the text 'new folder' and type in a meaningful name - ideally the name of the group of documents you are saving into this folder.

Moving Files

Moving files is a bit like cut and paste. To move files, open your File Explorer.

In the left hand pane, click the folder where the file you want to move, is saved, eg documents. Then click on the file(s) you want to move to select them. Hold down the ctrl key while you click to select multiple files.

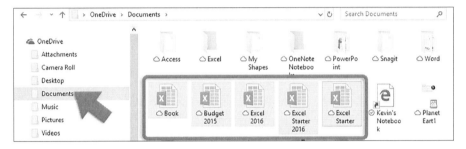

From the home ribbon select 'cut'.

Using the left hand pane, navigate to the folder you want to move the file to, eg documents > excel. Click the small down arrows to open the folders. Click the folder you want to move the files to.

Select 'paste' from the home ribbon.

Copying Files

Copying files is a bit like copy and paste. To copy files, open your File Explorer

In the left hand pane, click the folder where the file you want to copy, is saved, eg documents. Then click on the file(s) you want to copy to select them. Hold down the ctrl key while you click to select multiple files.

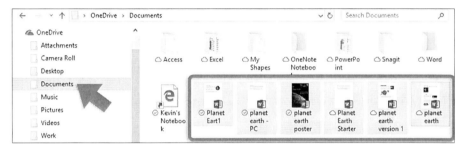

From the home ribbon select 'copy'.

Using the left hand pane, navigate to the folder you want to move the file to, eg documents > word. Click the small down arrows to open the folders. Click the folder you want to move the files to.

Select 'paste' from the home ribbon.

97

Apps & Applications

As mentioned earlier, applications are pieces of software that can be quite large and were originally designed to run on a desktop computer; you use the application using a keyboard and mouse.

Examples applications are Microsoft Office Suite: Word, Excel, PowerPoint, Adobe Creative Suite: Photoshop, Adobe Premiere and so on.

On the setup above, we have Microsoft Word running on a desktop computer.

You interact with the system using a keyboard and mouse, so the application and its interface is designed with this in mind.

This is an example of a desktop application. This application could also be running on a laptop.

A more recent incarnation of software is the App. Apps are usually smaller in size and are designed with a touch screen in mind. In the demo below, we have a maps app running on a tablet.

You interact with the system using your finger to manipulate the screen directly using a number of finger gestures; point, drag, tap etc. The interface is designed with this in mind, making icons bigger to enable you to tap on them with your finger.

Installing Apps

You can install apps from the Microsoft Store in Windows 10. Search for the app you want.

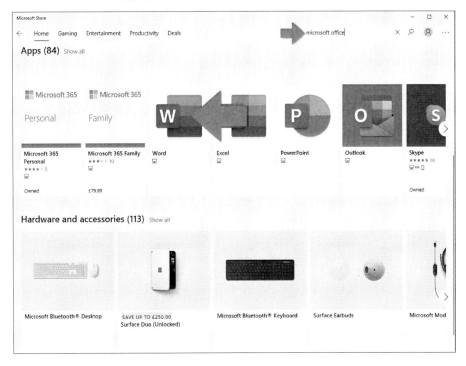

Select it from the search results. Click 'install'.

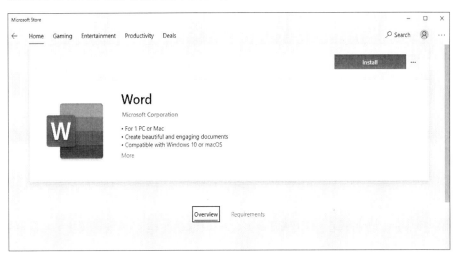

You'll find the app on your start menu.

Installing Software

Application software such as Adobe Creative Cloud, Microsoft Office or Libre Office can be installed using the setup or installer program you download once you subscribe to the service or buy the application. If you've downloaded the setup program, you'll find it in your downloads folder in File Explorer. Here in this example, I've downloaded libre office which is a free alternative to Microsoft Office.

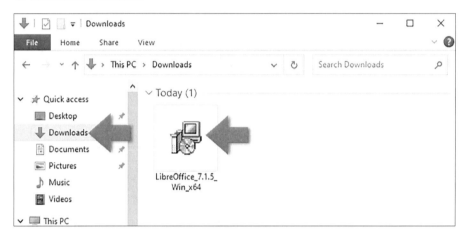

Run through the install routine.

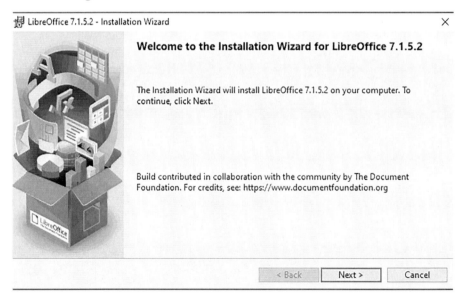

Once installed, you'll find the application on your start menu.

Some Useful Software

There is some useful software worth taking note of. Let's take a look...

Google Docs

Google's online word processing app allows you to create documents for free. A useful alternative to Microsoft Word. You'll need a Google Account to use this service.

Open your browser, navigate to :

`docs.google.com`

Google Sheets

Google's online spreadsheet app allows you to create spreadsheets for free. A useful alternative to Microsoft Excel.

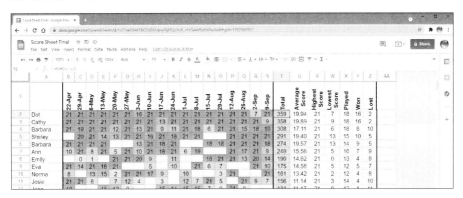

You'll need a Google Account to use this service. Open your browser, navigate to :

`sheets.google.com`

Chapter 3: Computer Software

Google Slides

Google's online presentation app allows you to create presentations for free. A useful alternative to Microsoft PowerPoint. You'll need a Google Account to use this service. Open your browser, navigate to :

```
slides.google.com
```

Libre Office

Libre Office is a good free alternative to Microsoft Office and is a software application you can download and install on your computer. Open your browser, navigate to :

```
www.libreoffice.org/download
```

Click 'download', then click on the setup program that appears on the bottom left. If it doesn't appear, go to your downloads folder, double click on LibreOffice_x.x.x_Win_x64.msi. Once installed, you'll find libre office on your start menu.

GIMP

A useful free image manipulation and editing program that is similar to Photoshop. Open your browser, navigate the following site and download the app:

```
www.gimp.org/downloads
```

Audacity

Audacity is a free audio editing application. You can record and edit audio files, as well as save MP3s etc. Open your browser, navigate the following site and download the app:

```
www.audacityteam.org/download
```

Zoom

Zoom is a video conferencing app and is useful for keeping in touch with friends, or collaborating with colleagues. Open your browser, navigate the following site and download the app:

```
zoom.us/download
```

Software Compatibility

If you are trying to install and run an older application, it may not run correctly under Windows.

Right click on the app on the start menu, go down to 'more', select 'open file location'.

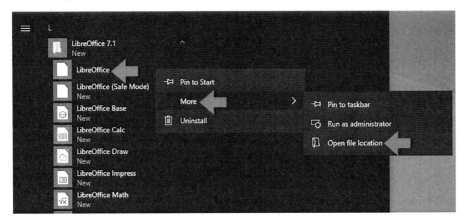

Right click on the shortcut, select 'properties' from the popup menu.

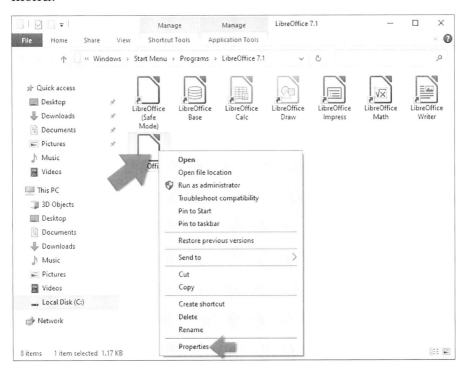

Select the 'compatibility' tab. If you're not sure what to select click 'run compatibility troubleshooter', this will analyse the program and pick the best settings. Run through the wizard then click 'test program'.

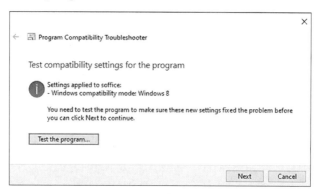

If you know what the specification for the program is, select them from the options. Eg if the program was designed for Windows 7, select it from the 'compatibility' mode section.

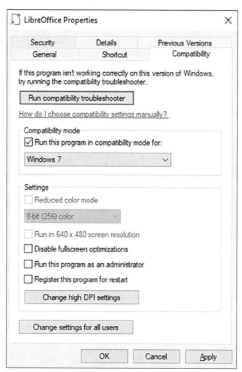

Now when you run the program, Windows will switch modes to accommodate the program.

Un-installing Software

There are two ways you can remove programs, through the control panel or directly from the start menu.

For desktop apps such as anti-virus software, Microsoft Office, Adobe Creative Suite and similar apps, you should remove these from the 'programs and features' section of the Control Panel.

As an example, I am going to remove 'avast antivirus' from my computer.

Right click on the start button, select 'apps & features

Scroll down the list, select the application you want to remove. Click 'uninstall'.

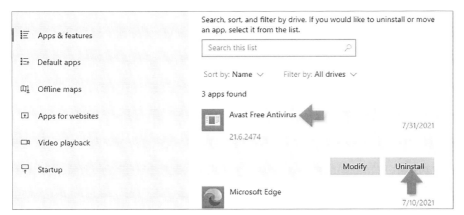

Click 'uninstall' on the confirmation dialog box to begin.

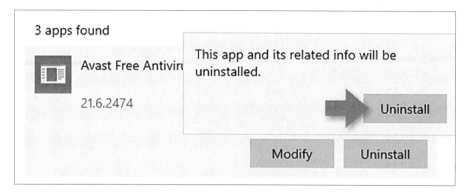

Now, depending on what program you are trying to remove, you might get a screen asking you what you want to do. In this case, avast is giving me options of what I can do.

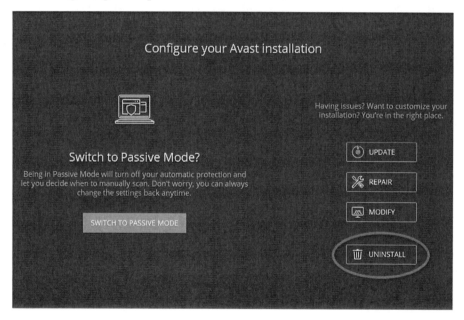

In most cases you just have to click the 'uninstall' button, also sometimes labelled 'remove'.

Once you have done that, the install wizard will run and start to remove the software you have chosen.

Depending on what you have chosen to remove, you might need to restart your PC.

This is a similar process for removing old versions of Microsoft Office or Adobe Creative Suite and any other desktop applications.

It's good practice to go through the apps and programs installed on your device, and remove the ones you don't use anymore and any old apps. This helps to keep your device running smoothly.

For apps that you have downloaded from the App Store and ones that come with Windows 10, you can remove them directly from the start menu.

To do this, right click on the icon on the start menu and select 'uninstall'. Tap and hold your finger on the icon, if you are using a touch screen tablet.

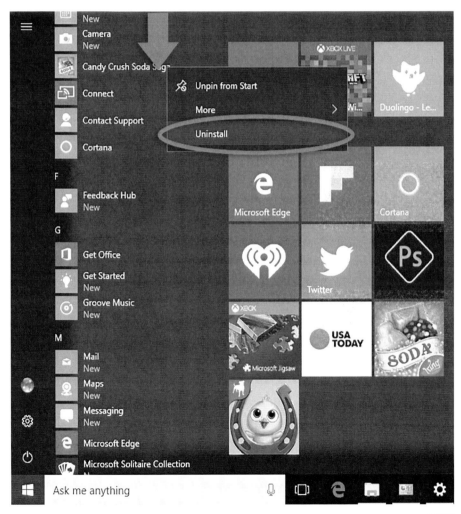

Resetting Apps

Sometimes apps can become slow and unresponsive, so in Windows 10, you have the option to reset the app. This will clear all the App's data, history lists, caches, settings and so on. This doesn't clear any of your personal files etc.

Settings App -> Apps -> Apps & Features.

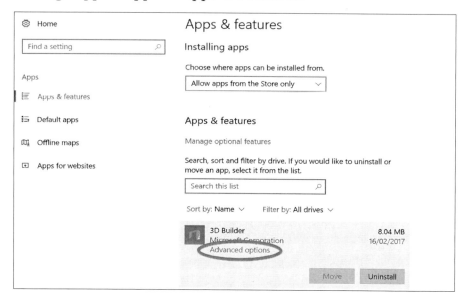

Tap on an App in the list, then tap 'advanced options'.

From the advanced options, tap 'reset'. Then tap 'reset' again to confirm.

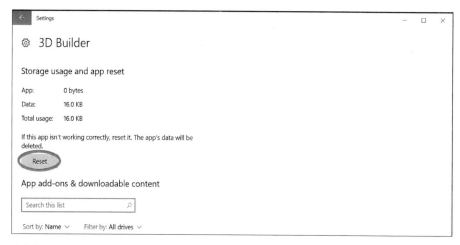

Start-Up Programs

Start up programs automatically start when you start up Windows - this can cause Windows to become very sluggish during start up. These are usually 'helper' apps that are installed with certain pieces of software and most can be disabled without any problem. Go to your settings app, select 'apps'. From the list on the left hand side, select 'start-up'.

On this screen you'll see a list of apps that are configured to start when Windows starts. Click the sliders next to each app to either enable or disable them - you can turn then on or off.

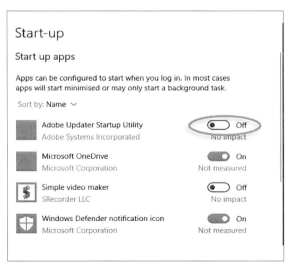

Arranging Windows on Desktop

It's useful when working in Windows 10 to arrange the windows on your desktop, especially when you're using more than one application at a time. For example, you could be browsing the web and writing a Word document at the same time- perhaps you're researching something, you could have Word open and your web browser next to it on the screen.

Moving a Window

Move your mouse pointer to the top of the window.

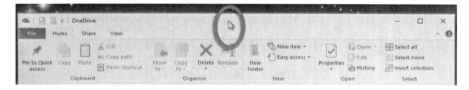

Now click and drag the window to your desired position on the screen.

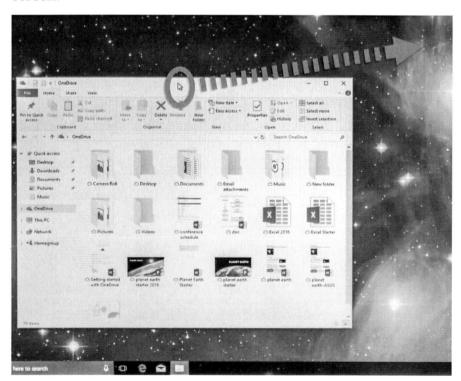

Resizing a Window

To resize a window, move your mouse pointer to the bottom right corner of the window - your pointer should turn into a double edged arrow.

The double edged arrow means you can resize the window. Now click and drag the edge of the window until it is the size you want.

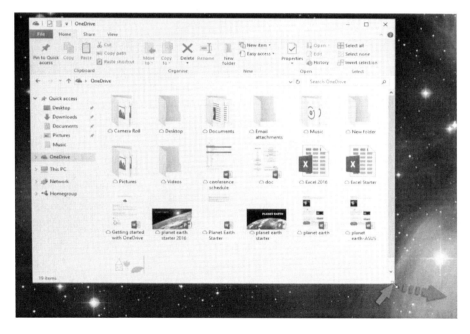

You can drag any edge of the window - left, bottom or right edge, but I find using the corner allows you to freely resize the window much more easily.

If you're on a touch screen, tap and drag the corner of the window.

Minimise, Maximise & Close a Window

On the top right hand side of every window, you'll see three icons. You can use these icons to minimise a window, ie reduce it to the taskbar essentially hiding the window from the desktop. With the second icon, you can maximise the window so it fills the entire screen, or if the window is already maximised, using the same icon, restore the window to its original size. The third icon you can use to close a window completely.

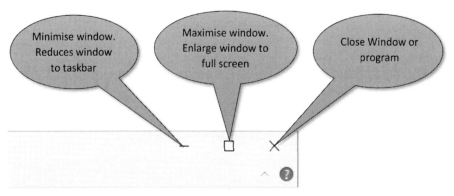

Window Snap Feature

The snap feature allows you to organize the windows on your screen. You can 'snap' them into place allowing you to put two app windows side by side. To do this, open an app, then click the title bar of the app and drag your mouse pointer to the edge of your screen.

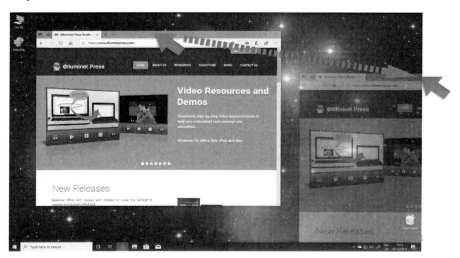

An highlight box will appear to show you where the window will snap to once you release your mouse button.

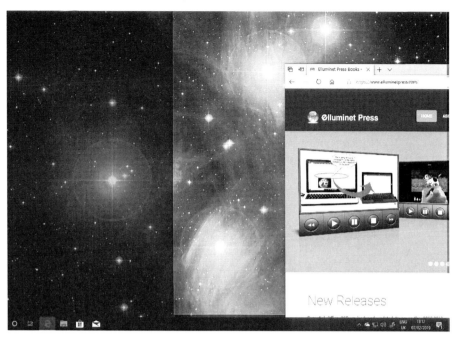

Once you let go of your mouse button, the window will snap into position.

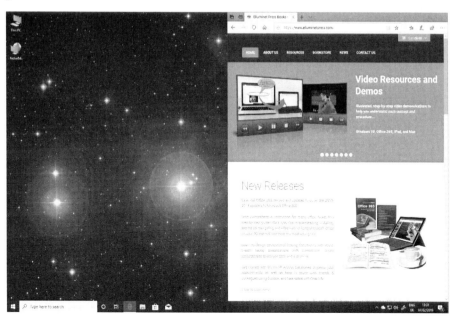

Internet Security

Security is important these days with the rise of cyber crime, phishing, and data theft.

In this chapter we'll take a look at some of the most common threats on the internet today, as well as some social engineering techniques used to trick users into handing over sensitive information.

We'll also take a look at some security and prevention methods that can be used to combat common threats.

Let's begin by taking a look at some of the different types of malware that are around.

Malware

Malware such as worms, viruses, and trojans are designed and written to exploit various different vulnerabilities in computer systems, particularly the operating system and web browsers in order to destroy data, take over a computer, or steal sensitive information.

Virus

A computer virus is a piece of malicious code that replicates itself by injecting code into other programs.

Worm

A worm is a standalone, self replicating, malicious computer program designed to cause disruption to a network, steal data, install a back door, or even lock files in a ransomware attack.

Trojan

The name and concept was derived from the story of the Trojan horse used to invade the city of Troy.

A trojan masquerades as an ordinary program or utility that carries a hidden, more sinister function. This could be data theft, or a ransomware attack.

Rootkit

A rootkit is a program designed to enable unauthorised, remote administrator access to a computer by opening a backdoor.

Rootkits don't replicate themselves like worms and viruses do and are usually installed through phishing scams, executable files, or software downloaded from a dodgy website.

Once installed, an attacker can connect to the infected machine and introduce other malware to steal information. Rootkits usually hide themselves on the infected machine and can be difficult to detect.

Ransomware

Ransomware is a malicious program designed to encrypt and lock a computer system until a fee is paid effectively holding the system to ransom.

Ransomware attacks are usually carried out using a trojan worm that a user is tricked into opening. These trojans can arrive through email or from a phishing scam.

The infamous wannacry worm, shown below, attacked the British National Health Service (NHS), where hospitals had to turn away patients or cancel scheduled appointments as many of the machines the NHS relied on became un-usable.

This is why it is important to keep regular backups of all your important data, and to never open attachments in suspicious looking emails that either come out the blue, or look like they've come from someone you know but the email wording doesn't quite sound like them.

Spyware

Spyware is a malicious program designed to discretely install itself onto your computer and gather information about you. This could include usernames and passwords, email monitoring, website browsing habits, credit card numbers, and other payment details. This information is then posted to a third party.

Social Engineering

Social engineering is the use of deception and manipulation to trick individuals into handing over confidential information such as passwords, bank details, and personal information in order to steal money or the person's identity.

Phishing

Pronounced 'fishing', this social engineering technique is designed to trick a user into handing over confidential information. Many phishing scams come via an email or phone call, that appear to originate from a legitimate source such as a bank, the police, IRS (HMRC), or a well known company. Here's one I received a few weeks ago.

The subject title usually tries to purvey some kind of imminent threat. While this may be used by genuine emails, but if it's pressuring you to take action then be suspicious of these emails.

The email above appears genuine and is designed to scare you, but if you hover your mouse over the links, you'll notice they have been spoofed. The link in the email doesn't match the destination site.

Also notice that the email has a generic greeting: "dear valued customer". Most genuine emails will address you by name.

The best advice is if in doubt, is never click on any of the links in an email, always go directly to the company's website using your browser, where you can check its authenticity. Phone the company using a trusted number to confirm it.

Following the link will take you to a fake website that looks exactly like the real thing, but notice the URL is fake... Barclays bank's domain name isn't `barclays-bank.uk`, it's `barclays.co.uk, barclays.com,` or `home.barclays.`

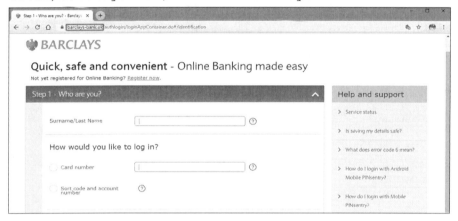

Pharming

Pronounced 'farming', this social engineering technique is designed to redirect a legitimate website's traffic to a duplicate fake site by either using the infected computer's hosts file, the victim's internet router, or a compromised DNS server. Using the fake site, the scammers can harvest usernames and passwords entered by unsuspecting users, then use them to gain access to the victim's accounts on the official website.

Install a good Anti-virus or Anti-malware program to protect yourself.

Pretexting

This social engineering technique uses a fabricated scenario designed to gain a user's trust and trick them into handing over personal information.

This scam is usually a phone call that appears to come from an authority such as the police or tax office, but could also impersonate a co-worker, an insurance company, some fake organisation running bogus special offers, or some external IT support company. Ignore them and hang up. Phone the organisation using a trusted number to check - don't use the number the scammer gave you.

Shouldering

Shouldering is a social engineering technique used to harvest passwords, PIN numbers and other sensitive data by discretely looking over someone's shoulder while they enter the information.

A typical scenario is a thief looking over someone's shoulder when using a cash machine, or when entering a pass code to unlock a phone or computer. So watch your back!

Tech Support Scams

These usually come as a phone call and is a form of social engineering designed to make you think your computer is infected with a virus or some other disastrous problem, when it actually isn't. The scammer then tries to extort money from you to 'fix' it. Ignore these idiots and just hang up!!

Fake Popup Messages

These usually appear when browsing the web and are designed to make you install malware, buy fake anti virus programs, or call a bogus support line. Don't fall for it! Don't click any links or buttons on the popup. Close the popup and ignore it. If it wont close,

press `control alt delete`, select task manager, right click on the browser, select 'end task'. Then run a malware/virus scan.

Threat Prevention

There are various countermeasures that can be employed to reduce the risk of attack or data theft.

Biometric Measures

New phones, tablets, and laptops nowadays, include finger print scanners, iris, and facial ID cameras, that use a finger print, or a mathematical representation of your face.

Strong Passwords

Instead of using easy to guess passwords like 'password123', your birthday, or child's name, you should choose a password that has nothing to do with you, or not even a real word. Use a mixture of upper and lower case letters, a number or two, and a couple of symbols such as an underscore_, or a dollar sign $. The more characters you use, the more difficult the password is to crack. You should also make passwords between 8 and 12 characters long. I can't stress the importance of strong passwords enough!

2-Factor Authentication

Many online services are starting to include 2-factor authentication where a confirmation code is sent to the user's phone number or email address that was registered when the account was opened.

Public Key Cryptography

Public key cryptography, also known as asymmetric cryptography, is an encryption scheme that uses two non-identical keys - a public key and a private key.

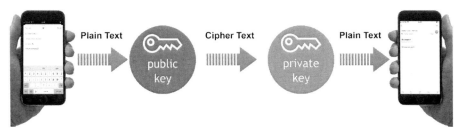

Public keys can be shared freely and are used to encrypt a message. Only users with the private key can decrypt the message.

This scheme is widely used in SSL and HTTPS to establish secure connections for websites, and also in the generation of digital signatures, and certificates.

Here is a digital certificate used to secure a website using SSL.

121

Firewalls

A firewall is a device or software program that monitors network traffic going into and out of a single computer or a network.

A firewall could be a software program installed on a computer. Windows 10 has its own firewall built into the operating system. This monitors data flowing in and out, as well as connection attempts.

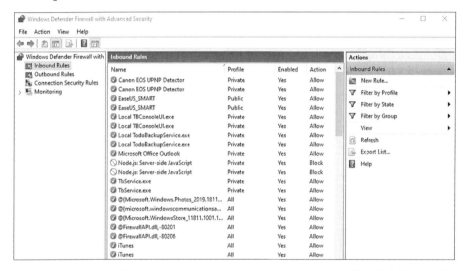

You can see in the screenshot above, windows defender firewall. You'll see a list of inbound and outbound rules. This is where you configure the firewall to allow or block traffic from various services and apps installed on the computer.

Routers

These days most domestic internet connections connect to the internet using a router. The first thing you should do once you connect your router to the internet, is change the admin password, as most default passwords are basic and are available online. Check the documentation that came with the router on how to do this. Anyone with the admin password can log into your router and compromise it's security.

Because of this problem, many manufacturers now automatically generate a random password and print it on the back of the router making things a bit more secure.

Anti-Virus Software

A lot of this software is sold pre-installed on the machine you buy and is offered on a subscription basis. So you have to pay to update the software. Don't buy it! There are plenty of safe free options to choose from, including Microsoft's Windows Security. You only need to install one piece of anti virus software, here are three you could use.

A feature to look out for is real time protection. This constantly monitors your machine for suspicious activity and blocks certain harmful content. If you use an email program such as Outlook, Windows Mail App, or Thunderbird, you might also want to consider email protection which scans incoming emails for potential threats.

Windows Security

Windows 10 comes pre-installed with Windows Security, formerly known as Windows Defender, is Microsoft's free anti-virus software. It does a decent job at protecting your machine and is frequently updated by Microsoft.

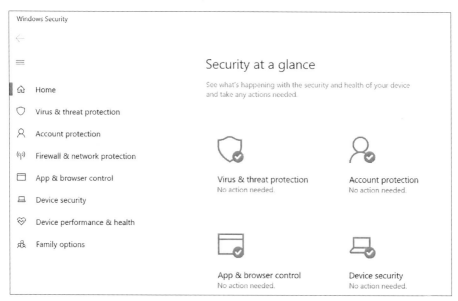

Three free ones that are a good place to start are Avast, AVG, and Sophos. These packages are very good. The free one is basic, but you can upgrade if you need something more.

Chapter 4: Internet Security

Avast

Avast scans and detects vulnerabilities in your home network, checks for program updates, scans files as you open them, emails as they come in and fixes PC performance issues.

You can download it from their website.

`www.avast.com`

Scroll down the page until you find 'download free protection'.

The other two versions here are 30 day trials and will expire after 30 days. You will need to pay a subscription to continue.

When prompted hit 'install'. If the installation doesn't run automatically, go to your downloads folder and run 'avast_free_antivirus_setup.exe', follow the on screen wizard.

AVG

AVG blocks viruses, spyware, and other malware, scans web link, as well as email and facebook links, and warns you of any malicious attachments.

You can download it from their website.

`www.avg.com`

Scroll down and click 'free download'.

The other versions here are 30 day trials and will expire after 30 days. You will need to pay a subscription to continue. The free version is good enough for home users.

Dealing with Infections

If you are running an antivirus program with real time protection, the system will prompt you with a warning if it has found a threat.

You can delete the file if it's an attachment from an email. Select 'clean', or 'heal' if it's a system file or part of a program. If you delete the file, the program may not work anymore. If in doubt, you can also quarantine the file, or 'move to vault' - this moves the file to an isolated area controlled by the antivirus program.

Using the Internet

The Internet is a global system of interconnected computer networks linked together using the TCP/IP protocol, and evolved from a research project to develop a robust, fault-tolerant communication network back in the 1960s, known as ARPANET.

Today, you can connect to the internet in a variety of different ways. Many of today's Internet Service Providers offer a DSL, Cable or Fibre Optic connection to the internet, depending on where you are.

Getting Online

There are 3 main types of internet connection: DSL, Fibre Optic and Cable. There are others, but they are less common.

Let's go through the most common options and see how they work.

DSL

Stands for Digital Subscriber Line and is basically implemented as **a**DSL, meaning the download speed is faster than the upload speed. This type of internet connection connects via your telephone line, allowing you to use both your phone and internet at the same time using a DSL filter.

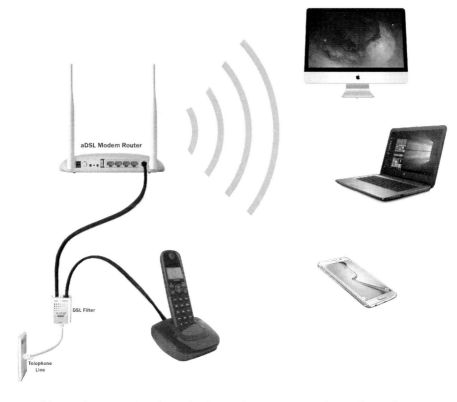

You'll need an **a**DSL / **a**DSL2 modem router that plugs into your phone line. These are usually supplied by your ISP, so check with them before buying.

Fibre Optic

In some countries, the fibre optic cable runs from the exchange to the telephone cabinet in your street and uses **v**DSL over the copper phone line to run the last 100-300m or so to your house.

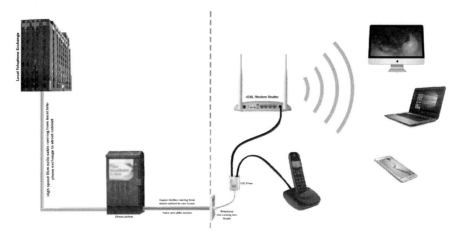

This is called FTTC or 'fibre to the cabinet' and has a very similar setup to the illustration above.

For this option to work you will need a modem router that is compatible with **v**DSL/**v**DSL2. Check with your ISP for specific details.

If you're lucky enough to can get fibre running directly to your home, this is called FTTP or 'fibre to the premises' and is set up as shown below.

This means the fibre optic cable runs from the exchange all the way to your house.

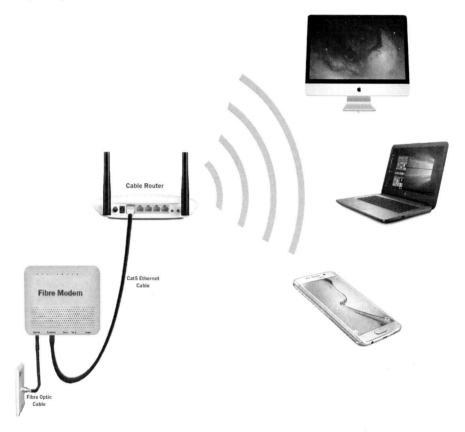

The fibre optic cable will plug into a modem supplied by your ISP which will connect you to the internet.

You can then buy a cable router that has WiFi capabilities and plug that in using an ethernet cable. This will allow you to have WiFi in your house.

Some ISPs will already have this built into their modem, so check with them first.

All your devices such as your laptop, computer, phone, and tablet will connect to the internet through your modem.

Cable

Cable Internet is distributed via your cable TV provider and usually runs down a COAX cable rather than a phone cable.

Setups may vary slightly from different providers, however most will be similar to the one illustrated below.

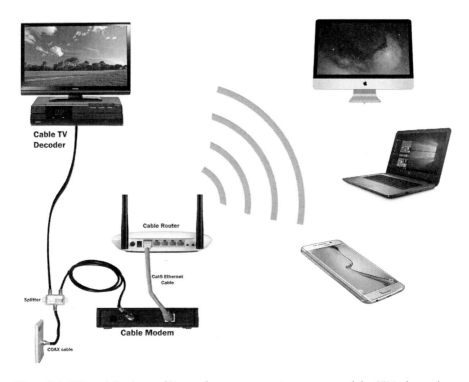

The COAX cable is split and one goes to your cable TV decoder and the other to your cable modem. From your cable modem, you can connect a cable router using an ethernet cable, which can provide WiFi. Some ISPs will already have this built into their modem, so check with them first.

Satellite

This option is available in rural areas where line based broadband services such as DSL or Fibre aren't available.

It uses a satellite dish to provide access but speeds tend to be lower and weather conditions can interfere with reception.

3G/4G/5G

This option uses the mobile/cell phone network and usually involves plugging a USB dongle with a SIM card into your computer.

3G and 4G are usually included with smart phones as part of your package or contract.

Speeds have improved over the years, however they are still very slow in comparison with DSL, Cable or Fibre Optic.

Browsing the Web

To browse the web, you need a web browser. There are various browsers such as Firefox, Edge and Google Chrome. Google Chrome is a fast and streamlined browser that is a good alternative to Microsoft Edge. To use Chrome, you'll first need to download it. You can download Google Chrome from

`www.google.com/chrome`

Hit the 'download chrome' button. Click 'accept and install'. Go to your downloads folder and double click 'chromesetup.exe'

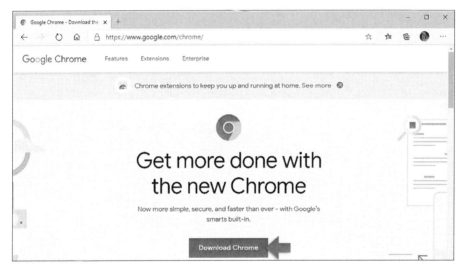

Follow the on screen instructions to install the browser. You'll find Chrome on your start menu and on your desktop.

Once Chrome has loaded, click the profile icon on the top right and enter your Google account username and password.

This is the same account that you use for Gmail if you have one.

You can use Chrome without a Google account, but you won't get any of the personalised features or be able to add apps to Chrome from the Chrome Store.

This is Chrome's Home screen. You can type in your Google Search or type a URL if you know it into the search bar. Along the bottom you'll also see your most visited websites.

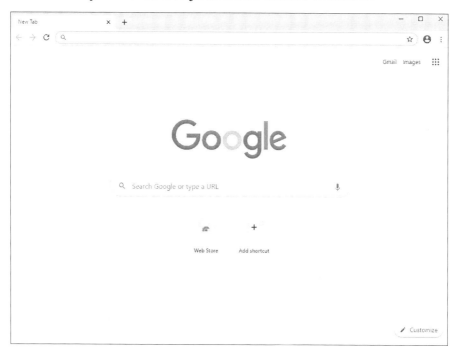

Let's take a closer look at Chrome's interface.

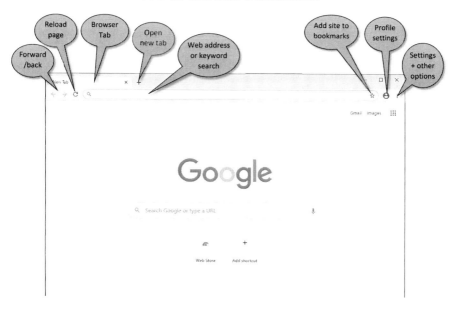

Google Search

Google is a search engine that allows you to search for websites, photos, videos, products and pretty much anything else you can thing of. Google works with keywords, you can type these into the search bar in Chrome

Web Addresses

Each web site on the World Wide Web has an address called a URL or Uniform Resource Location. Such as:

www.elluminetpress.com
www.google.com

The URL itself can be broken down into its basic elements. Lets take a closer look at an example.

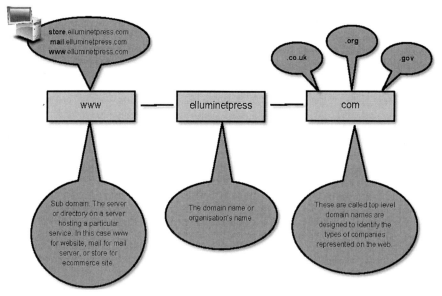

The URL starts with either HTTP or HTTPS, however most modern browsers hide this, and you don't need to include it when typing in a URL. This is known as Hypertext Transfer Protocol. HTTPS is encrypted and you'll want to make sure the websites you're visiting use this protocol. You can tell by looking at the address bar. If the site is using HTTPS, then you'll see a padlock on the left.

www means the server hosting the service, in this case www for World Wide Web. Usually points to the public_html directory on the web server where the website's files are stored.

elluminetpress is the domain name or organisation's name and is unique to that organisation.

.com is the type of site. It can be **.co.x** for country specific companies (eg .co.uk), **.org** for non profit organisations, **.gov** for government organisations, or **.com** for commercial company. These are known as top level domain names and are designed to identify the types of companies represented on the web.

Anything in the URL after the domain name, points to a specific page, or directory on that website. For example

www.elluminetpress.com**/resources**

Bookmarks Bar

The bookmarks bar is where you can save websites. The bar shows up just below the address bar at the top of the screen. I'd advise you to only pin the websites you use most often to this bar, otherwise it can get a bit cluttered.

To enable the bookmarks bar, click the 'three dots icon' on the top right of the screen, and select 'bookmarks' from the menu.

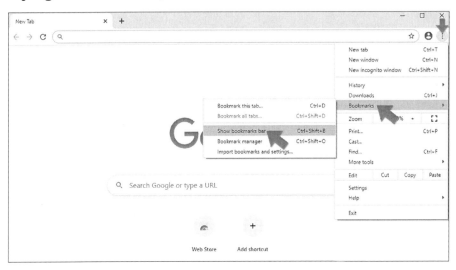

Click 'show bookmarks bar' to enable it.

Add Website to Bookmarks Bar

To add a website, first navigate to the page you want to add, then click the star icon on the top right of the address bar.

In the dialog box that appears, type in a meaningful name for the website.

Click on the drop down box next to 'folder'. Select 'bookmarks bar' to add the website to the bookmarks bar, or select the folder you want to save the website into.

Click 'done' at the bottom of the dialog box.

Organising the Bookmarks Bar

You can organise your bookmarks into folders. This helps keep sites of the same genre together. For example, you could have a folder called 'work' for all your business sites, a folder called 'social' for all your social media, or a folder for any interests you have eg gardening or photography. Create these on your bookmarks bar for easy access.

To create a folder, right click on the bookmarks bar, select 'add folder'.

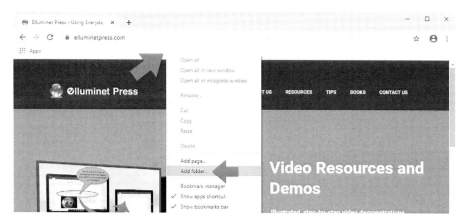

Type in a meaningful name for the folder, eg: 'work'.

You'll see your folder appear on the bookmarks bar.

You can click & drag any bookmarks into the folder.

Click on the folder name to open it up

Browsing History

Chrome keeps a list of every website you visit. To find your browsing history, click the three dots icon on the top right. Select 'history', then click 'history' on the slide out menu.

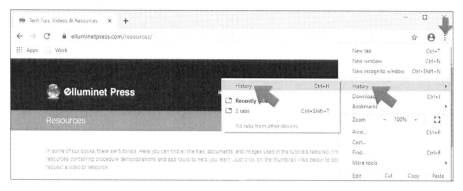

You'll see a list of the sites you've visited. Click on a site to revisit.

You can also see a list of sites you've visited while you've been browsing if you click and hold your mouse pointer on the back icon.

Click any of the links to return to the website.

Finding Files you've Downloaded

Whenever you download files from a website, you'll find the files in your downloads folder.

To open your downloads folder, click the 'three dots icon' on the top right of the screen, and select 'downloads'

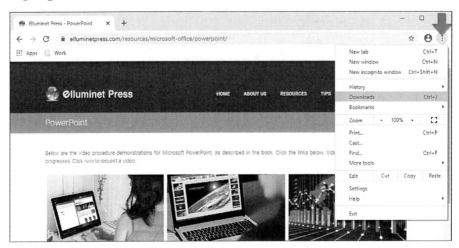

Here, you'll see a history list of all the files you've downloaded. To open or run any of these downloads, double click on the link in the list.

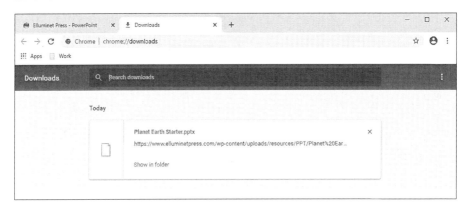

To open your downloads folder in File Explorer, click 'show in folder'. From File Explorer, you can double click on the file to open it or run it.

To delete the download from your list, click the x on the right hand side of the download item in the list.

Printing Pages

To print a web page, click the three dots icon on the top right of the screen, then select 'print' from the drop down menu.

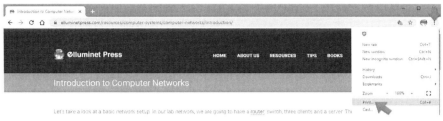

From the panel on the right hand side, select the printer. Under 'copies', enter number of copies if needed.

Under 'layout', select portrait or landscape. Under 'pages', enter the page numbers you want to print. You'll see the page numbers in the print preview on the left if you scroll down the page.

Click 'more settings' on the bottom left. From here you can print background graphics, add or remove headers and footers, or print more than one page to a sheet of paper, and change the paper size.

141

Extending Chrome

Extensions are small apps that add functionality to the chrome browser. To see what extensions are installed on your chrome browser, click the three dots icon on the top right. Select 'more tools', then click 'extensions' from the slide out menu.

You'll see a list of any extensions that are installed. To add new extensions, click the hamburger icon on the top right.

Select 'open chrome web store' on the bottom left.

In the web store, you can search for an app.

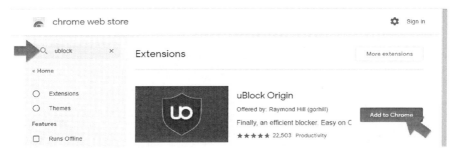

Click 'add to chrome' to install the extension

Using Email

There are two ways you can access your email. You can sign up and use an online service such as Gmail, Yahoo, or outlook; or you can use a mail app such as Windows Mail App, Microsoft Outlook, or Mozilla Thunderbird.

Web Based Mail

If you're using Gmail, Yahoo, or hotmail/outlook, then you can check your email using your web browser.

For Gmail, go to:

```
mail.google.com
```

For Yahoo mail, go to:

```
mail.Yahoo.com
```

For hotmail or outlook, go to:

```
outlook.com
```

Windows Mail App

Web based email is fine if you only have one email address, but if you have two, then checking multiple accounts is more difficult. Windows has a built in mail app where you can add your email addresses.

You'll find the mail app on your start menu.

When you start the app, you'll be asked to add your Microsoft account. If you don't have a Microsoft account, go to the following site and create one.

```
signup.live.com
```

This will create you an account with an email address

Chapter 5: Using the Internet

Adding your Email Accounts

If you have another email account such as Gmail or Yahoo you can add these too.

To do this click the settings icon on the bottom left of the screen.

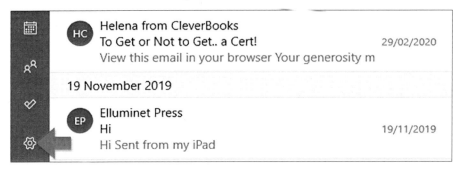

Click 'manage accounts' on the side panel on the right hand side of the screen.

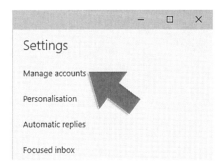

Click 'add account'.

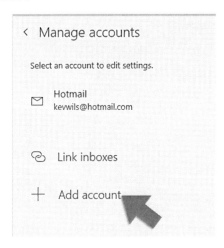

Select the account provider. Eg if you are adding a Gmail or Google account, click 'Google', if it's Yahoo, click 'Yahoo', or Apple, click 'iCloud'.... If your provider isn't in the list above click 'other account'.

In this example, I want to add my Gmail account. So I'd select Google.

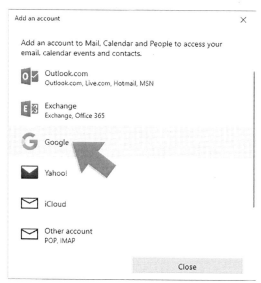

In the 'connecting to a service' dialog box, type in your email address for the email account you're adding. Click 'next'.

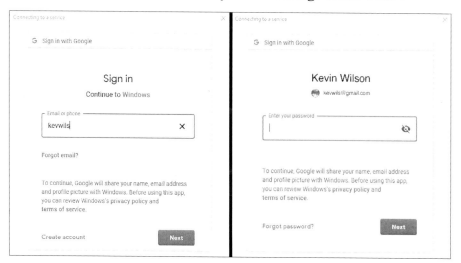

Enter your password on the next screen, click 'next'.

In the next window, scroll down and select 'allow' to give Windows permission to access your account. Then click 'done'.

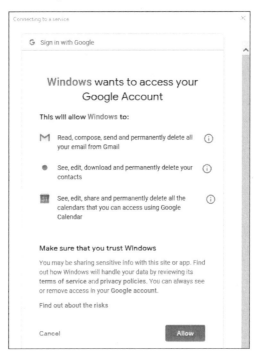

All your email accounts will appear under the accounts section on the left hand side of the screen. Click the hamburger icon on the top left of the screen to reveal the full sidebar.

Reading Mail

When you open mail app it will check for email, any new messages will appear in your inbox.

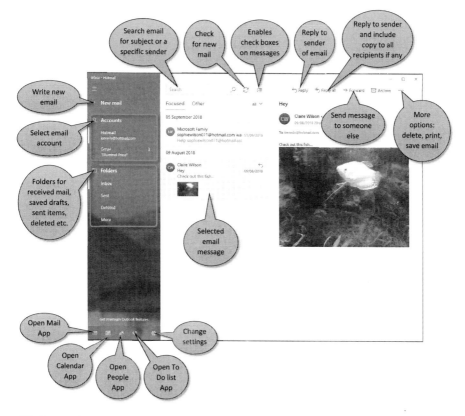

Click on the message in your inbox. The contents will be displayed in the reading pane on the right hand side.

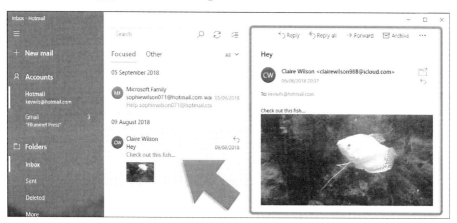

Mozilla Thunderbird

To use Thunderbird, you'll first need to download it. Open your browser and go to the following website

`www.thunderbird.net`

Click on 'free download'. Double click on the 'thunderbird setup' that pops up on the bottom left of your screen. If it's not there, go to your downloads folder and run the setup from there.

Run through the setup wizard to install the software.

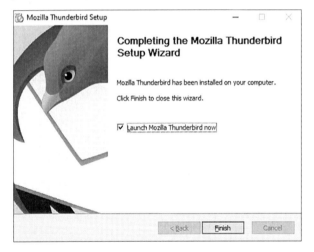

Add your email address and password, click 'continue'.

Once you've added your address, you'll land on the home screen. You'll see your email account listed down the left hand side. Here, you'll find your inbox and set items. In the top pane, you'll see a list of emails, in the bottom pane you'll see the email you've selected. This is called the reading pane.

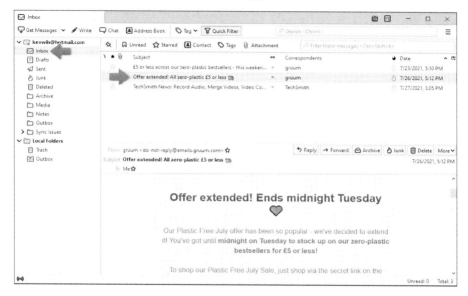

To reply to a message, select the message from the top pane, click reply.

To write a new message, click 'write' on the top left. Enter the person's email address, then type your message.

Cloud Computing

The "cloud" was originally a metaphor for the internet, and many network diagrams represented the internet with a symbol of a cloud.

The Cloud

As internet services advanced, the cloud became a set of hardware devices including data servers and application servers that provide services such as email, apps and disc storage for documents, music and photos.

These cloud services include the delivery of software and remote storage space having as little as possible stored on the user's machines.

If you have an account with a web-based e-mail service like Hotmail or Gmail, then you've had some experience with the cloud. Instead of running an e-mail program on your computer, you log into a web e-mail account remotely.

The storage for your account doesn't exist on your computer, it's on the cloud. In this example, files would be stored on OneDrive and if you're using Google, your files would be stored on GoogleDrive.

You can run Microsoft Word online using your tablet, laptop or phone to edit your documents. If you are using GoogleDrive, you can use GoogleDocs to edit your document. All these can be used through a web browser on your device. These are called web apps.

You can also collaborate with other users, colleagues or friends. You can share photos or documents for them to see and edit; working on projects together around the world, or just share the latest photo with a friend.

This has become a huge advantage as data can be stored centrally making backups easier. Applications and servers can be built and maintained centrally by dedicated support staff making downtime a minimum.

Your files on the cloud are stored on a server in a server farm rather than locally on your computer. In the photograph below, there can be about 20 or more servers stacked up in each cabinet and hundreds of cabinets filling entire rooms serving millions of people who subscribe to the service.

OneDrive

OneDrive is a cloud file hosting service and synchronises your files between your device (pc, laptop, phone or tablet), and the cloud file hosting service.

You'll find OneDrive in your File Explorer window. Click the icon on your taskbar to open.

OneDrive is where you should save all your files from Microsoft Office, photographs, music, videos and so on. The advantage is, if your computer crashes, you won't lose all your files as they will still be stored on OneDrive.

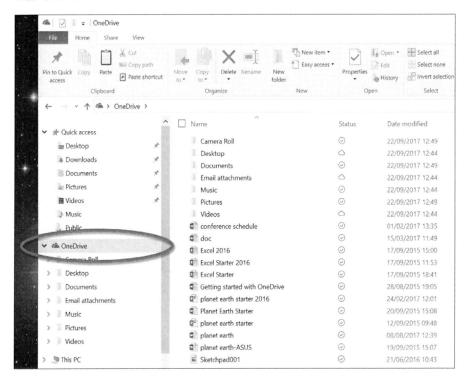

The other advantage of OneDrive, is you can access all your files on all your devices. So you can see your documents on your PC, phone, tablet or laptop, and you can access them from anywhere that has an internet connection.

Google Drive

To access Google Drive on the web, open your web browser, then navigate to the following website.

`drive.google.com`

You'll need a Google account to use Google Drive. If you use Gmail, sign in with your email address and password.

If you don't have a Google Account, you'll need to create one.

`accounts.google.com`

Once you sign into Google Drive using your web browser, you'll land on the home screen. Let's take a look. Down the left hand side panel you'll see some options.

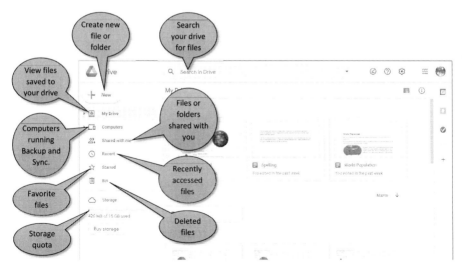

In the main screen, you'll see your 'my drive' view with a list of all the files and folders you've saved to your drive.

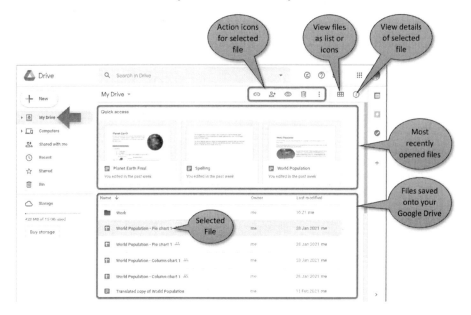

If you select a file, you'll see an icon panel appear on the top right. Here, you can create a shareable link, share the file, preview the file or delete the file.

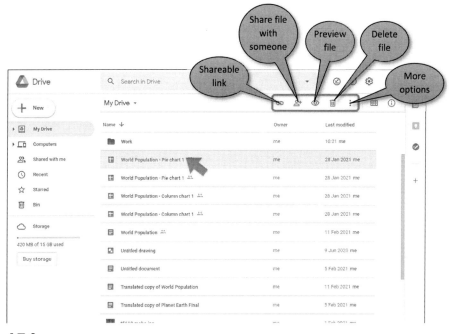

Select the 'more options' icon and you can open the selected file with another app, add a shortcut to your drive sidebar, move the file to another folder, make the file available offline, rename the file, view the file's details, make a copy and download the file for use in another application such as Word, Excel, etc.

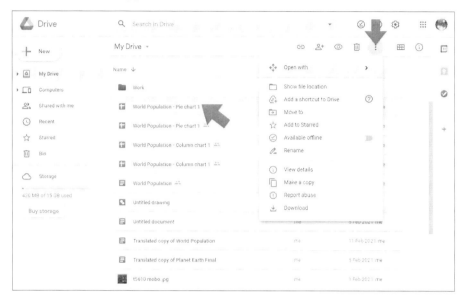

Have a look at Backup & Sync on page 163 to synchronise your files with Google Drive in File Explorer.

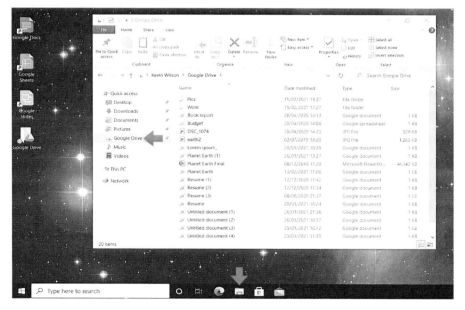

Backing Up

If you have ever lost data because of a computer glitch or crash you know how frustrating it can be. So we all need a good backup strategy.

Windows 10 has a built in backup utility called FileHistory that allows you to select files and back them up to an external hard drive.

You can also backup your files to OneDrive, Google Drive, or a NAS drive.

Creating a Local Backup

The first strategy is to use FileHistory in Windows 10 to create a local backup on an external hard disk drive.

Setup

First of all go buy yourself a good external hard disk - go for at least 1TB. This is a small device that plugs into a USB port on your computer.

Plug in your external drive into a free USB port.

Chapter 6: Backing Up

In the search field on the task bar type 'backup'.

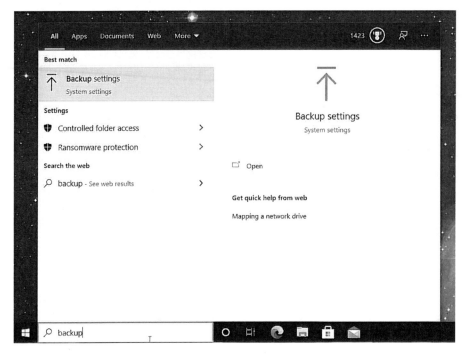

Click 'backup settings' from the search results.

On the screen that appears, click the switch in the "backup using file history" section to enable File History, if it isn't already.

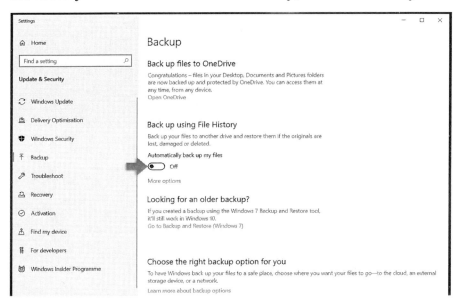

Click the add drive icon, then select your external drive from the popup list.

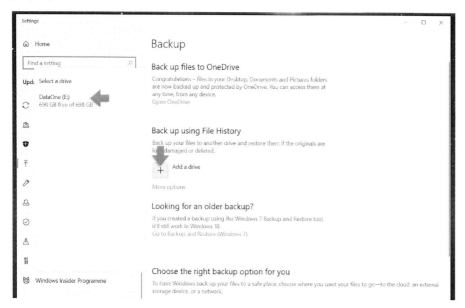

Once you have turned on File History, Windows 10 will start to backup your files (documents, pictures, music etc) onto your external hard drive.

If you want to add folders, just add the folders to your backup. Remember your desktop, documents, photos, music & videos folders and their contents are already included.

To do this, click "more options"...

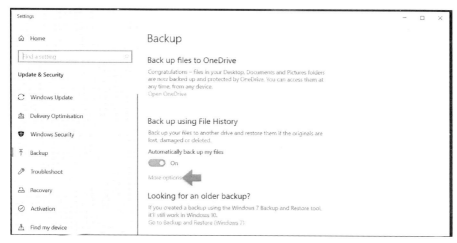

Select the "add a folder" icon.

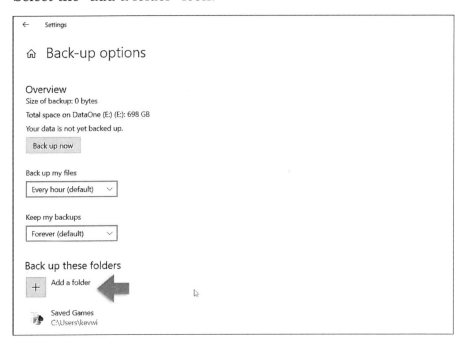

Navigate to and select the folder you want to include in the backup.

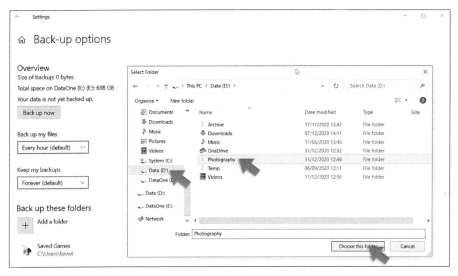

This folder will now be backed up with the rest of your folders.

Click "backup now" to force a new backup.

Scheduling Backups

By default, File History saves files every hour, but you can change this by clicking on "more options" in the backup settings

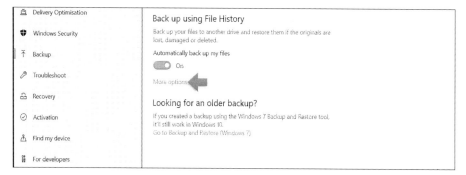

Select an option from the "backup my files" drop down menu

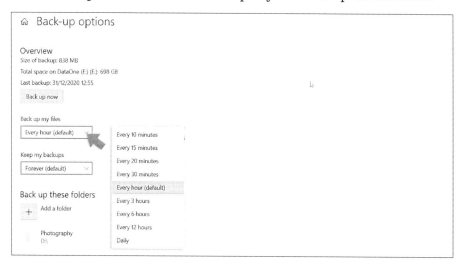

A good guide is to set how often File History saves files to "Daily". This will tell File History to save copies of your files once a day. For most users this is sufficient.

Set 'keep my backups' to 'until space is needed'. This means that File History will keep creating backups while there is sufficient space on the hard drive, then once the drive fills up, File History will start to delete the oldest backups to make space for new backups. Good practice would be to plug in your external drive at the end of each day to back up what you have done throughout the day.

Restoring Files

Plug in your external Hard drive. Type 'Restore Your Files' into the search field on the bottom left of the screen. Select "restore your files with File history" from the search results.

Use the left and right arrows at the bottom to navigate to the date backed up when you know your file still existed or was working.

Then in the library section double click in the folder the file was in eg pictures if you lost a photo.

Select the photo and to restore it click the green button at the bottom of the window.

Google Drive

With Google Drive, you get 15GB free, so you can backup your files to Google Drive. First, you'll need to download and install the Backup and Sync utility. To do this open your web browser and navigate to the following website.

```
www.google.com/drive/download
```

To install backup and sync, scroll down the installation web page to the 'individual' section. Click 'download'.

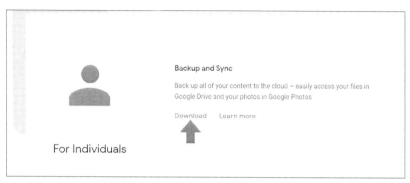

Click the download on the bottom left of your screen to begin. If you don't see a prompt, you'll find the utility in your downloads folder.

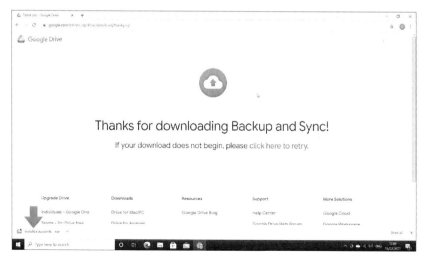

Follow the prompts on the screen to begin the setup. The utility will download and install on your computer. After a few seconds, you'll see the install wizard appear.

Chapter 6: Backing Up

Click 'get started'

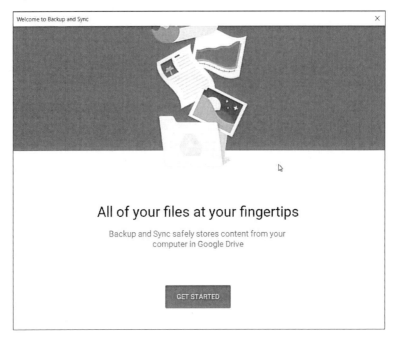

Sign in with your Google Account email address and password.

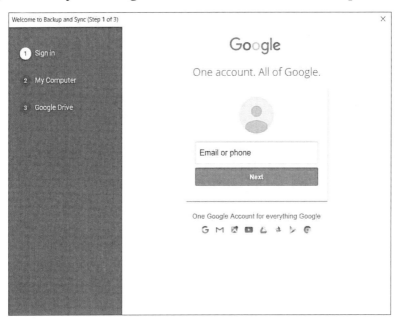

Click 'next'.

Select any folders on your computer you want to backup to Google Drive. This could be your documents folder, pictures, or any folder you save files to. These folders appear in the 'computers' section on Google Drive.

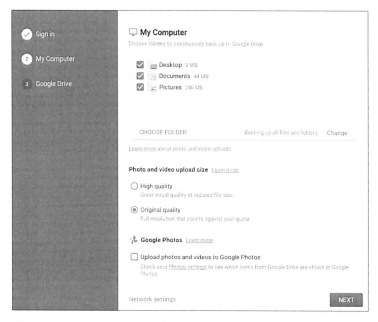

If any folders you use don't appear, click 'choose folder' then select the folder to add. You don't have to select any folders to backup and you can untick all the suggestions if you don't want to backup files. Click 'next'.

Select 'sync my drive to this computer'. Most of the time you can leave this in the default location, but if you need to change the folder or drive Google Drive syncs files to, select 'change' then choose a folder.

Select 'sync everything in my drive', then click 'start'.

You'll notice some icons appear on your desktop, these are shortcut icons to Google Drive, Docs, Sheets, etc.

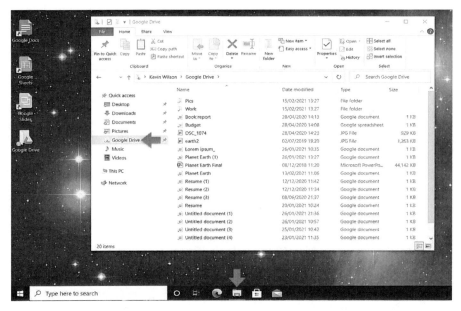

You'll also find the Google Drive folder in File Explorer. This is where you should save new files that you want to sync across to Google Drive and be available on all your devices.

You'll also see the backup and sync utility in the system area on the bottom right of the screen. Here you can view recently synced files as well as change settings.

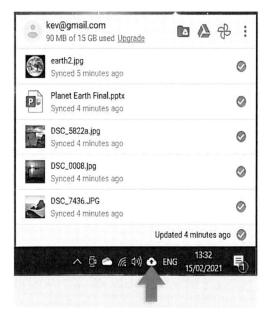

The icons along the top of the window allow you to view Google Drive folder in File Explorer, open Google Drive in a web browser, open Google Photos.

The three dots icon on the top right, will reveal a drop down menu, where you can change settings, pause sync, or change account.

NAS Drives

Network Attached Storage drives such as Synology Diskstation or WD My Cloud offer a good backup solution, especially if you have a lot of files.

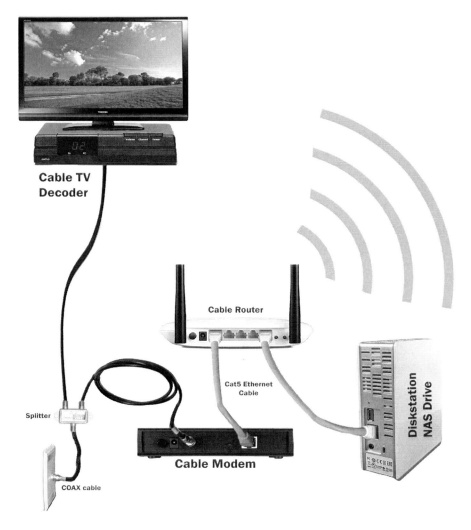

You plug the NAS drive into your router using an Ethernet cable, then you install a backup and sync utility such as Synology Drive Client on your computer.

The backup process is similar to Google Drive except it backs the files up to the NAS drive.

Common Problems

Computers are complex pieces of equipment which means there are a lot of things that could potentially go wrong.

It could be a problem with the hardware, an app, or driver, or even Windows itself. So whatever is causing the problem, troubleshooting is a process of trial and error in order to isolate the problem.

Here is a checklist of the first steps I usually take when troubleshooting certain problems. If these steps don't work, then you know there is a more serious problem that requires a re-install or new hardware.

Computer Won't Turn On

- Check that the power cables are plugged into a power socket and the socket is turned on.

- Try using a different power socket.

- If you're in the UK, check the fuse in the plug.

- Try a different power cable.

- Check the monitor is plugged in and turned on.

- Check the monitor cable is plugged into the back of the machine, and into the monitor itself. This is either a VGA, HDMI, or DVI cable (as shown below).

- Check the brightness & contrast levels of the monitor, make sure it hasn't been set too dark.

- If you're on a laptop, check the battery, check the power adapter is powered on and plugged in. Allow the battery to charge. If the battery was depleted to 0%, some devices wont start unless they have had a chance to charge the battery.

Keyboard or Mouse not Working

- Make sure the keyboard or mouse is firmly plugged into the back of the computer

- Try plugging your keyboard or mouse into a different USB port.

- On your keyboard press the Caps Lock key. If you don't see the indicator LED light up it may be a dead keyboard.

- Check the optical sensor on the underside of your mouse, it may need a clean.

- If you are using a wireless keyboard or mouse, try recharge or replace the batteries.

- If it is a bluetooth mouse or keyboard, try re-pairing it with your computer.

Computer Freezes

- Press Ctrl Alt Del on your keyboard, then select 'task manager'. Click on the 'processes' tab. Right click on any programs with the status 'Not Responding', then select 'end task' from the popup menu.

- Try restarting your computer. Many simple problems can be resolved with a reboot.

- If you can't shutdown or restart your computer, hold down the power button until it turns off. Wait 30 seconds then turn it back on again.

- Scan for viruses and malware.

Windows Wont Start

If your computer turns on but Windows doesn't show up...

- This could be a driver problem. Has anything changed since the last time you successfully started Windows? Have you installed a new piece of hardware such as a video card, a new printer? Have you updated a driver? Try booting into safe mode. Then open 'apps & features' and un-install the software. Or open device manager to remove a driver. See page 181.

- Try repairing Windows. See page 183.

- Try restoring Windows to a previous restore point, if system restore was enabled. See page 184.

- It could be Windows itself, try refresh or re-install Windows. See page 185.

PC Boots Slowly

If your PC starts running slowly, there are a few things you can try to speed things up.

- Run virus/malware scan.

- Remove all the crap installed on your machine – ie programs and software you don't use. See page 105.

- Remove startup programs. See page 188.

- Defrag your drive. See page 189.

- Refresh your PC – this re-installs a fresh copy of Windows 10. This usually retains all your files, but backup your files anyway just in case. See page 185.

Slow PC

There could be various reasons your PC is running slowly.

- Press control shift escape to open task manager, go to processes, sort the list by CPU. See which process is taking up a high percentage of processing time. Right click, select 'end task'.

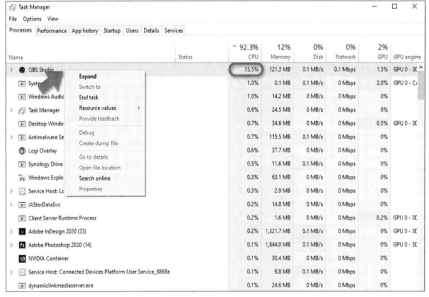

- Check your power settings. Right click on start button, select 'power options', click 'additional power options'. Select high performance, or balanced.

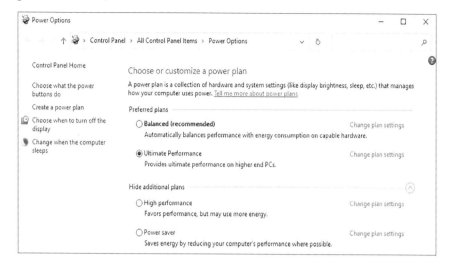

- Disable shadows, animations and visual effects. Type 'appearance and performance' into the search field on the bottom left.

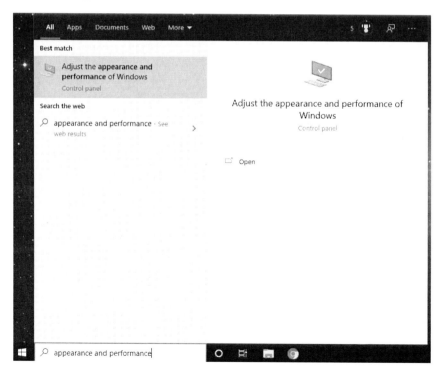

- Turn off the animations & visual effects as shown below. Click on the tick boxes to 'un-tick' the options.

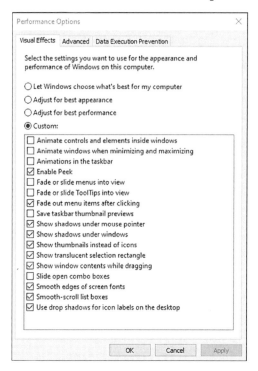

- Disable transparency effects. Open settings app, select 'personalisation', click 'colors'. Turn off the 'transparency effects' switch.

- Turn off background apps. Open settings app, select 'privacy'. Scroll down to 'background apps', turn off 'let apps run in background'.

- Run disk cleanup. See page 190.

- Check for corrupted Windows files. See page 187.

- Check your anti-virus software, there could be a scan running in the background. Stop the scan.

- Scan for malware.

- Refresh your PC – this re-installs a fresh copy of Windows 10. This usually retains all your files, but backup your files anyway just in case. See page 185.

No WiFi

These days a good WiFi connection is essential. Most of the time they're pretty reliable, but on occasion you might have problems. Here are a few steps you can take to help you troubleshoot the problem.

- If you're using a laptop, some machines come with a WiFi kill switch. If this is the case, make sure it is turned on.

- Check the WiFi status on the bottom right of your taskbar. You should see a wifi icon, if you see a globe icon, this means you're not connected to a network. Click on the icon and select your WiFi network.

 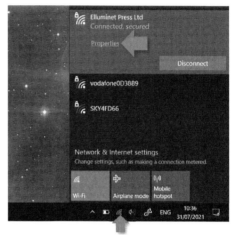

If you are connected, click on your WiFi connection, select properties. Scroll down to the properties section.

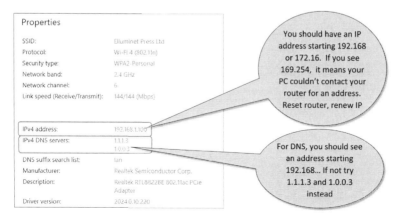

If you need to change the IP/DNS settings, type 'view network status and tasks' into the search field on the bottom left. Select 'view network status and tasks'.

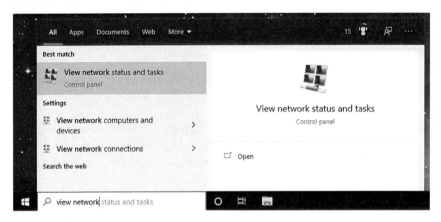

Click 'change adapter settings' on the left. Then right click on your WiFi adapter, select properties.

Select IP 4, enter any IP address or DNS settings.

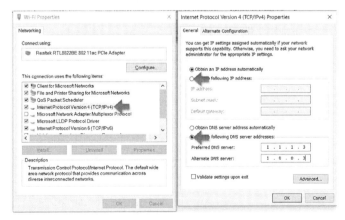

- Check WiFi network name and password are correct.

- Make sure your computer isn't in 'airplane mode'.

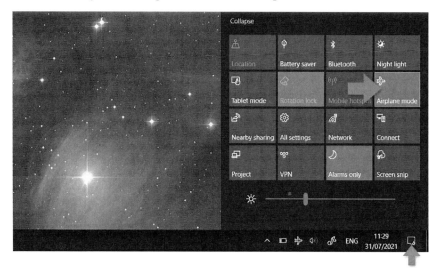

- Turn off your WiFi router and unplug it from the power. Wait 30 seconds, then plug it back in and turn it on. Wait for the router to connect. Check the lights on the router, make sure it connects to the internet. You'll find a description of what the lights mean in the booklet that came with your router - or ask your service provider. If it doesn't connect, there could be an issue with your connection. Contact your service provider.

- Try reinstall the WiFi adapter. Right click on start button, select device manager. Select 'network adapters'. Right click on the WiFi driver (marked 802.11) and uninstall it.

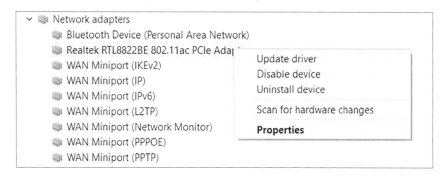

Restart your machine.

- Open the command prompt as an administrator - right click on start button, select 'windows powershell (admin).

Type the following commands. To reset the connection back to a clean state, type:

```
netsh winsock reset
```

To force your PC to give up its IP address lease, type:

```
ipconfig /release
```

To assign a new IP address to your PC, type:

```
ipconfig /renew
```

To reset TCP/IP stack back to its original configuration, type:

```
netsh int ip reset
```

To clear the current DNS cache, type:

```
ipconfig /flushdns
```

Restart your machine.

- Check your Anti-virus software isn't blocking internet activity.

Recovery Mode

If you're having trouble starting Windows, you can force windows 10 to boot into the recovery environment.

Entering the Recovery Environment

To do this, start your machine, then when you see the start up logo screen, hold down the power button until your screen goes blank.

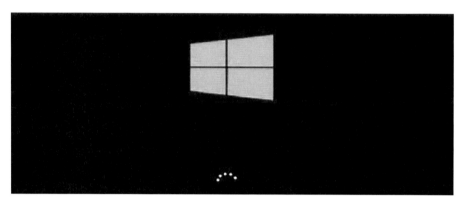

Wait a few seconds, then press the power button again to start your machine.

When you see the start up logo screen, hold down the power button again until your screen goes blank.

Wait a few seconds, then press the power button again to start your machine.

This time, allow your device to fully restart. You should see this screen.

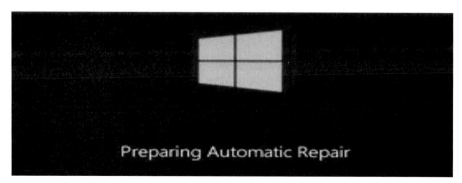

Once the WinRE environment starts, you'll see the 'automatic repair screen'. Click 'advanced options' to begin.

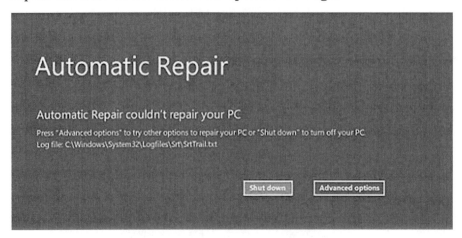

Click 'troubleshoot'.

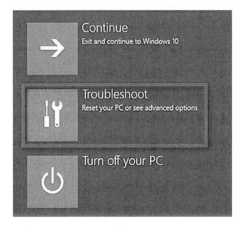

Click 'advanced options'.

Safe Mode

First, boot your computer or device into recovery mode. See page 179

From the advanced options, select 'startup settings'. Click 'reset'.

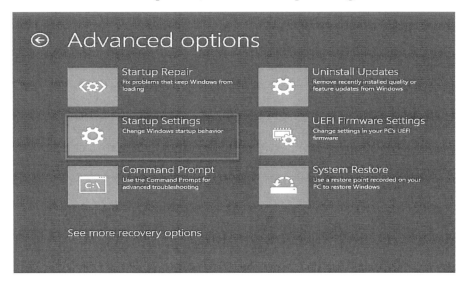

Press F4 to 'enable safe mode'.

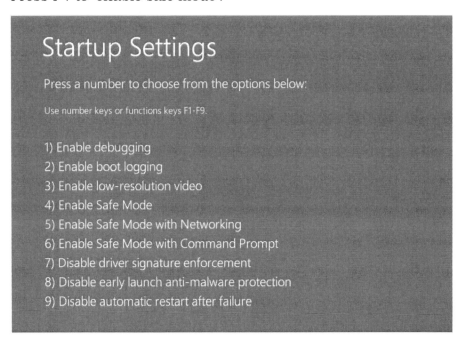

Your computer will boot into a stripped down version of itself. This means it won't load any drivers, startup programs, or apps.

Sign in as normal. From here, you can un-install drivers, or software that was causing the start up problem.

Right click on the start button. Here, you can get to apps & features to un-install software, or 'device manager' to uninstall a driver. As well as 'computer management', 'disk management', and the 'powershell', depending on what the problem is.

Reboot normally and try again.

Startup Repair

Startup Repair is a recovery tool that scans your PC for the problems that might prevent Windows from starting and then tries to fix them automatically, so your PC can start correctly.

To launch startup repair, first, boot your computer or device into recovery mode. See page 179

Select 'start up repair' from the advanced options.

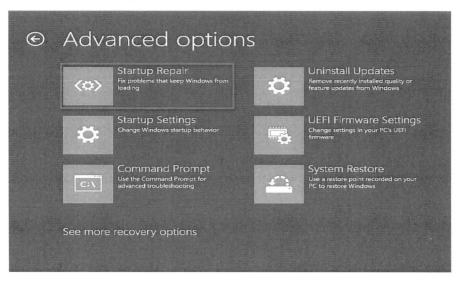

Select your Microsoft Account and enter your password.

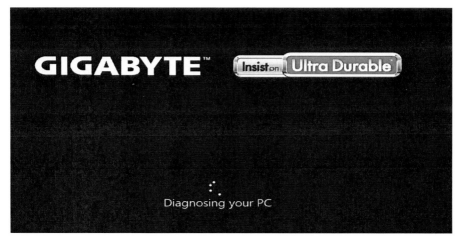

Allow the recovery software to analyse and attempt a repair.

Restore Point

To launch startup repair, first, boot your computer or device into recovery mode. See page 179

Select 'system restore' from the 'advanced options'.

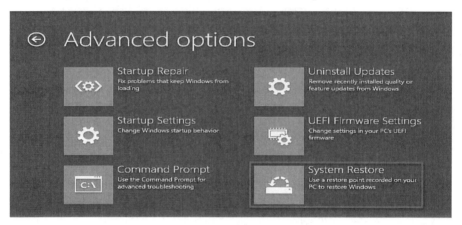

Select your Microsoft Account, then enter your password.

Run through the restore wizard, select the latest restore point.

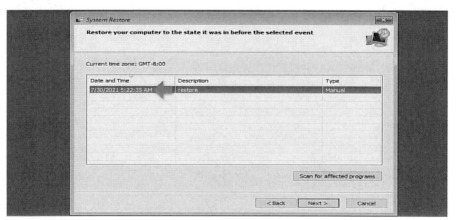

Re-install Windows

First, boot your computer or device into recovery mode. See page 179

From the 'troubleshoot' screen, click 'reset this PC'.

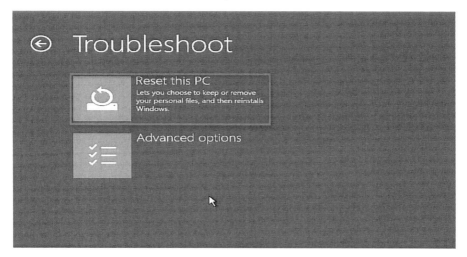

From here you can do a complete re-install by clicking on 'remove everything'. This will remove all your files and applications and reset Windows 10 back to its factory default.

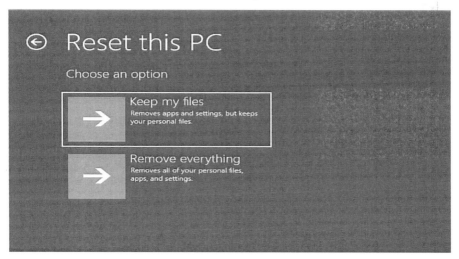

Click 'keep my files' to refresh Windows 10. This will delete all your installed applications and settings. Your personal files and data will remain intact.

Select where you want to download the installer from.

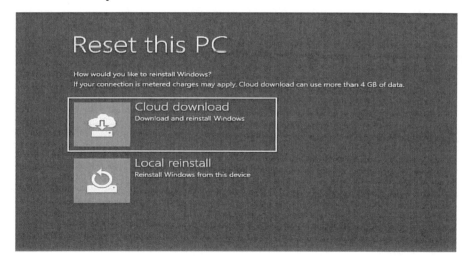

Click 'local reinstall' to reinstall Windows 10 from the recovery partition on your hard drive.

You can also download from the cloud meaning the installer will download the installer files from Microsoft's servers to re-install windows. Select this one if, the local install doesn't work and you are on the internet with a fast connection.

Click 'reset' to confirm your options, then allow the installer to re-install Windows.

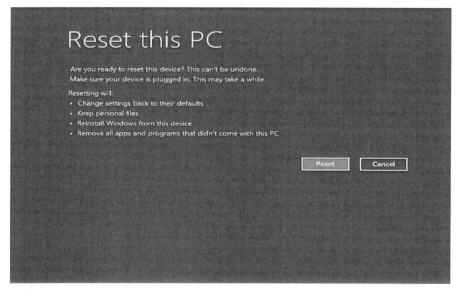

System File Check

This utility checks for corrupted system files and replaces them as necessary. To do this within Windows, open the command prompt as an administrator.

If you can't get into Windows, boot to the Recovery Environment, see page 179. Select 'command prompt' from the 'advanced options' screen.

Type the following command

```
sfc /scannow
```

SFC will scan your system files and replace any it finds to be corrupt.

```
Administrator: Command Prompt - sfc /scannow                    —   □   ×
Microsoft Windows [Version 10.0.19042.685]
(c) 2020 Microsoft Corporation. All rights reserved.

C:\WINDOWS\system32>sfc /scannow

Beginning system scan.  This process will take some time.

Beginning verification phase of system scan.
Verification 1% complete.
```

To check the log type:

```
notepad %windir%\Logs\CBS\CBS.log
```

This will open the log file in notepad.

```
Administrator: Command Prompt                                  —   □   ×
Microsoft Windows [Version 10.0.19042.685]
(c) 2020 Microsoft Corporation. All rights reserved.

C:\WINDOWS\system32>sfc /scannow

Beginning system scan.  This process will take some time.

Beginning verification phase of system scan.
Verification 100% complete.

Windows Resource Protection did not find any integrity violations.

C:\WINDOWS\system32>notepad %windir%\Logs\CBS\CBS.log

C:\WINDOWS\system32>
```

Startup Programs

Go to your settings app, select 'apps'. From the list on the left hand side, select 'start-up'.

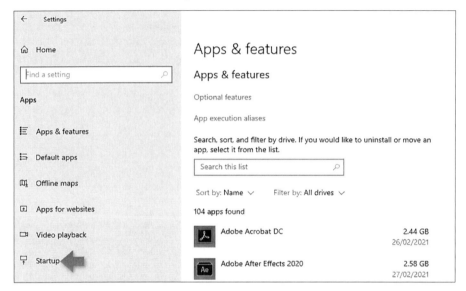

On this screen you'll see a list of apps that are configured to start when Windows starts. Click the sliders next to each app to either enable or disable them - you can turn then on or off.

Most of these programs can be disabled with the exception of your sound, video and network devices, Windows defender, and OneDrive.

Drive Optimisation

To de-fragment the disk in Windows 10, type 'defragment' into the search field on the taskbar. Click 'Defragment and optimise your drives'.

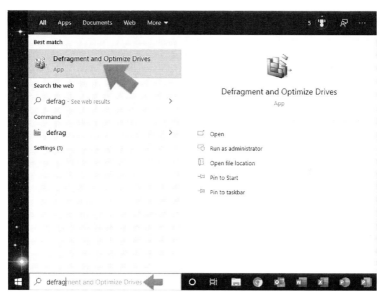

Select the drive you want to defrag. Click the 'optimize' button.

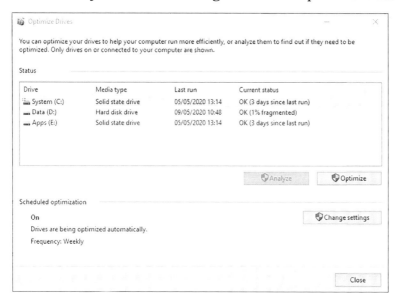

This will start de-fragmenting your disk. This process can take a while.

Disk Cleanup

Over time, windows gets clogged up with temporary files from browsing the internet, installing and un-installing software and general every day usage. Doing this once a month will help keep things running smoothly.

Type 'disk cleanup' into the search field on bottom left the taskbar.

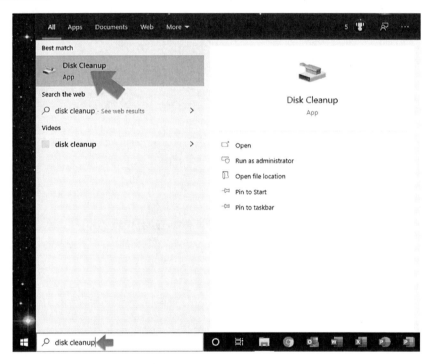

Click 'clear disk space by deleting unnecessary files'

Select drive C, click ok.

In the window that appears you can see a list of all the different files and caches. It is safe to select all these for clearing.

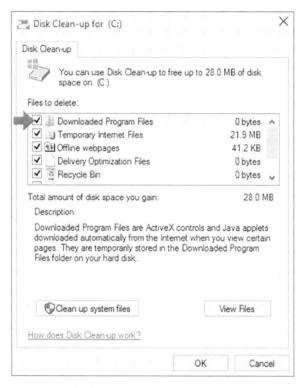

Once you are done click ok and windows will clear out all those old files.

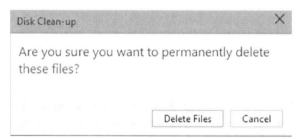

Click 'delete files' on the confirmation dialog box to clear out all the old files

Do the same with the system files. In the window above, click 'clean up system files'.

This helps to keep your system running smoothly. A good rule of thumb is to do this about once a month.

Further Reading

To further your skills using your computer, have a look at the following books.

You'll also find Windows 10 video demos and tutorials here

    www.elluminetpress.com/win-10

Office demos and tutorials

    www.elluminetpress.com/office

Computer basics tutorials

    www.elluminetpress.com/comp

    www.elluminetpress.com/peripherals

Windows 10 Fundamentals

For a more in depth understanding of Windows 10, try out Windows 10 Fundamentals.

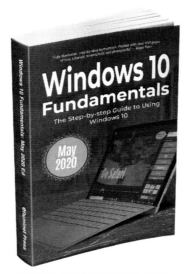

ISBN: 9798727083581

Exploring Microsoft Office

For a more in depth understanding of Microsoft Office Applications such as Word, Excel and PowerPoint, try out Exploring Microsoft Office.

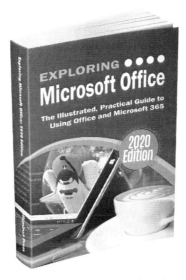

ISBN: 9781913151362

Index

Symbols

1/4" (6.35mm) Phono Jack 70
1/8" (3.5mm) Phono Jack 70
3G/4G/5G Internet 131

A

Action Centre 85
aDSL 127
Alt Key 56
Anti-Virus Software 123
  Avast 124
  AVG 124
  Dealing with Infections 125
  Windows Security 123
Applications 98
  Start-Up Programs 109
Apps 98
  Installing Apps 99
  Resetting Apps 108
  Start-Up Programs 109
  Un-installing Apps 105
Arranging Windows 110
  Moving a Window 110
  Resizing a Window 111
Audio Card 25

B

Backing Up 156
  Google Drive 163
  Local Backup
    File History 157
    Restoring Files 162
    Scheduling Backups 161
  NAS Drives 167
Browsing the Web 132

C

Cable Internet 130
Chrome 133
Close a Window 112
Cloud Computing 150
Components 20
Component Video 69
Composite Video 69
Computer Freezes 171
Computer Types 13
  All-in-one 14
  Chromebook 17
  Desktop 13
  Hybrids 19
  Laptop 15
  Netbook 16
  Tablets 18
Computer Won't Turn On 169
Control Key 56
CPU 20
CTRL 56

D

Defrag Drive 189
Disk Cleanup 190
Disk Defrag 189
Domain Name 135
Double Click 52
DSL 127
DVD Drive 59
DVI 67

Index

E

Email 143
 Mozilla Thunderbird 148
 Web Based Mail 143
 Windows Mail App 143
  Adding your Email Accounts 144
  Reading Mail 147
eSATA 66
Ethernet 65
Expansion Slots 24
External Drive 57

F

Fibre Optic 128
File Explorer 92
 Copying Files 97
 Creating Folders 95
 Home Ribbon 93
 Moving Files 96
 Organising your Files 94
 Share Ribbon 93
 View Ribbon 93
File Management 94
Firewalls 122
FireWire 65
Flash Drives 57
Freezes 171
FTTC 128
FTTP 129

G

Getting Online 127
Google Chrome 133
 Add Website to Bookmarks Bar 136
 Bookmarks Bar 136
 Browsing History 139
 Extending Chrome 142
 Finding Files you've Downloaded 140
 Google Search 134
 Organising the Bookmarks Bar 137

Printing Pages 141
Google Drive 153
Graphics Card 26

H

Hard Disk 22
HDD 22
HDMI 68
HTTPS 121

I

IEEE 1394 65
iLink 65
Initial Setup 74
Internet 126
Internet Security 114

K

Keyboard not Working 170
Keyboards 55
  Cursor Keys 57
  End Key 57
  Function Keys 56
  Home Key 57
  Modifier Keys 56
    Alt 56
    CTRL 56
    Shift 56
    Win 56

L

Left Click 52
Live Tile 83

M

Malware 115
Managing your Files 94
Maximise 112
Memory 21
Minimise 112
Mobile Internet 131

Index

Monitors 27
Motherboard 23
Mouse 50
  Double Click 52
  Left Click 52
  Right Click 52
  Scroll Wheel 53
  Using the Mouse 51
Mouse not Working 170

N
NAS Drives 61
nit 30
No WiFi 175

O
OneDrive 152
Operating System 73
Optimise Drive 189

P
PCIe 24
PCI express 24
PC Sluggish 172
PC Starts Slow 172
Pen Drives 57
Pharming 118
Phishing 117
Phono Jack 70
Play DVD 59
Popup Messages 119
Pretexting 118
Printer Drivers 46
Printers 33
  Add Printer to Windows 10 40
  Connection Problems 41
  Connect using Ethernet 45
  Connect using USB 45
  Inkjet 33
  Installing Printers 36
    Brother Printers 39

    Canon Printers 39
    Download the Printer Drivers 46
    Epson Printers 38
    HP Printers 36
  Laser 34
  Managing Printers 48
  Older Printers 42
  Print Quality Problems 49

Q
QWERTY 55

R
RAM 21
Ransomware 116
RCA Audio 71
Recovery Environment 179
Re-install Windows 185
Resolution 28
Restore Points 184
Right Click 52
RJ45 65
Rootkit 115
Router Security 122
Running Windows the First Time 74
  Advertising ID 80
  Connect to your WiFi 75
  Enter WiFi Password 76
  Find my Device 79
  Improve Inking & Typing 80
  Link your Phone 77
  Meet Cortana 78
  Regional Settings 74
  Send Diagnostic Data 79
  Set a PIN Code 77
  Set Location 79
  Set up OneDrive 78
  Sign in for the First Time 76
  Tailored Experiences & Diagnostic Data 80
  Terms Of Use 75

S

Safe Mode 181
Satellite Internet 131
Screens 27
Scroll Wheel 53
SDD 22
Search 88
  Narrowing Down the Search 91
  Searching for Apps 90
  Searching for Files 89
  Searching for Windows Settings 91
SFC 187
Shared Folder 61
Shift Key 56
Shouldering 119
Slow Boot 172
Slow PC 172
Snap Feature 112
Social Engineering 117
Software 72, 100
  Installing 100
  Software Compatibility 103
  Some Useful Software 101
    Audacity Audio Editor 102
    GIMP Image Editor 102
    Google Docs 101
    Google Sheets 101
    Google Slides 102
    Libre Office 102
    Zoom Video Chat 102
  Un-installing Software 105
Solid State 22
Sound Card 25
Spyware 116
SSL 121
Start Menu 82
Startup Programs 188
Start-Up Programs 109
Startup Repair 183
System File Check 187

T

Task Bar 84
  System Icons 85
Threat Prevention 120
  2-Factor Auth 120
  Biometric Measures 120
  Strong Passwords 120
ThunderBolt 66
Timeline Activity History 87
Touch Pad 53
  Left Click on Something 54
  Right Click on Something 54
  Scroll 55
Trojan 115

U

UNC path 61
Un-installing Software 105
URL 134
USB 63
USB 2.0 63
USB 3.0 63
USB-C 64
USB Drives 57
USB Key 57
Using the Internet 126

V

VGA 68
Video Card 26
Virus 115
VLC 60
VLC Media Player' 60

W

Web Addresses 134
WiFi Problems 175
Windows Desktop 82
Windows Key 55
Window Snap Feature 112
Windows Recovery Environment 179

Index

Windows Wont Start 171
WinRE 179
Worm 115

X

XLR 71

Made in United States
North Haven, CT
26 October 2021